For Chris and Melissa McCarthy

TINTIN AND THE SECRET OF LITERATURE

Tom McCarthy

Granta Books
London

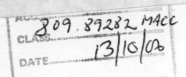
Granta Publications, 2/3 Hanover Yard, Noel Road,
London N1 8BE

First published in Great Britain by Granta Books 2006

The pictures are reproduced with kind permission of the following:
TNT en Amérique, Jochen Gerner, 2002. Courtesy of L'Ampoule. *Une Guerre du Pétrole* ('A Petrol War') from *Le Crapouillot*, 1920. *Haddock Goes to Heaven*, Simon English, 2005. Courtesy of FRED, London, LTD. Farinelli, the castrato (*née* Carlo Bruschi, 1705–82) by Bartolomeo Nazari, Royal College of Music. http://www.mystudios.com/gallery/forgery/history/ *The Balloonatic*, Buster Keaton and Edward F. Cline, 1923, *Keaton's Silent Shorts*, Oldham, S Illinois University Press.

A CIP catalogue record for this book is available from
the British Library.

1 3 5 7 9 10 8 6 4 2

ISBN-13: 978-1-86207-831-9
ISBN-10: 1-86207-831-4

Typeset by M Rules

Printed and bound in Great Britain by William Clowes Ltd, Beccles, Suffolk

CONTENTS

ACKNOWLEDGEMENTS

There are several people without whom this book would not have been what it is, or simply not have been at all. I am grateful to George Miller and and Sajidah Ahmad at Granta Books for helping to shape it; to Jonny Pegg and Shaheeda Sabir at Curtis Brown for helping secure funds to write it; to Simon Critchley for sharing his thoughts on simulacra, humour and economics in contexts both formal and in-; to my library pal Sally O'Reilly for putting me on to Paul de Man's essay 'The Rhetoric of Temporality'; to my mother, Penny, for first exposing me to Hergé's work when I was seven and the many people in dialogue with whom I have developed my ideas about Tintin, literature, or both since then; and to Eva Stenram, for being great.

1

R/G

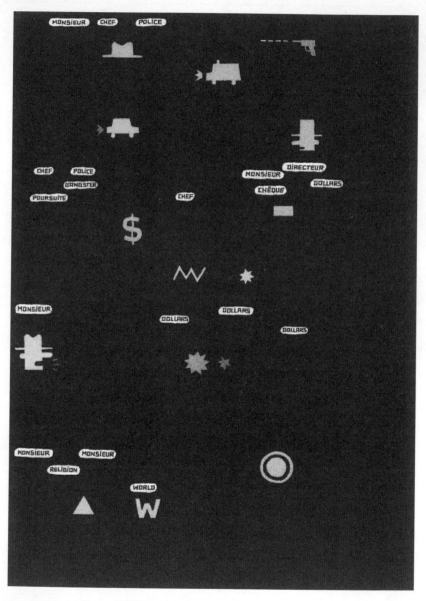

From *TNT en Amérique*, Jochen Gerner, 2002.

i

'At "*Le Petit Vingtième*" we are always eager to satisfy our readers and keep them up to date on foreign affairs. We have therefore sent TINTIN, one of our top reporters, to Soviet Russia. Each week we shall be bringing you news of his many adventures.' Thus began, on 10 January 1929, in the children's supplement of the Belgian newspaper *Le Vingtième Siècle*, the series of cartoons that over the next five decades would capture and hold the imagination of tens of millions of children aged, as their publishers would repeatedly boast, from seven to seventy-seven. Or rather, thus *almost* began: first there was a footnote, an addendum: 'N.B. The editor of "*Le Petit Vingtième*" guarantees that all photographs' – in the original French, *toutes ces photos*, 'all *these* photographs' – 'are strictly authentic, taken by Tintin himself, aided by his faithful dog Snowy!'

What a strange claim. The photographs that follow are patently not 'authentic', nor indeed are they photographs. In black and white line drawings we see the tufted reporter running around battling communists, crashing cars, trains, speedboats and planes, and even (for the first and last time) writing copy. Yet we are asked to believe that these images are, or at least 'represent', *photographs* of Tintin, taken *by* Tintin, and that these 'photographs' somehow manage to show him not, as you would logically expect, in the act of taking a photograph (pointing the camera at himself from arm's length and so on), but rather in the full throes of a series of actions so frenetic that any attempt to photograph them, let alone for their protagonist to do so, would be futile.

Well, you might say, this is just a playful ruse, a convention set in place to give the drawings context and direction. And of course you would be right. If, in addition, you knew a thing or two about the history of comics, you would point out that the medium was fairly new in 1929: Rudolph Dirk's *The Katzenjammer Kids* and George McManus's *Bringing Up Father* had been appearing in American newspapers since 1897 and 1913 respectively, but these were short, light-hearted skits, not extended adventures that laid claim to social and political insight. In order to meet these new demands being made of it, you would argue, the cartoon format needed to undertake a set of twists and shuffles that would allow it to invoke notions of documentary rigour while at the same time making no attempt to disguise the fact that it was all fictitious. In this, too, you would be right. But if you had your literary goggles on, a strange coincidence would strike you: this ruse, this hastily convened convention and these twists and shuffles mirror the ones carried out by another hybrid entertainment format that emerged several centuries before cartoons did: the novel.

Open most early novels and you will find, before the story

proper gets under way, an extremely dubious statement 'explaining' how the events of which you are about to read came to be known to the author. Writing against a new scientific background which demanded provable facts and an old theological one that deemed lying a sin, these seventeenth-century pioneers took great pains to tie their use of 'Invention' and 'Romance' to solid values of honesty and accuracy. They might argue, like Daniel Defoe, that truth can be better conveyed when 'insinuated under the guise of some Symbol or Allegory'; or they might claim, like John Bunyan, to be presenting accounts 'received from such hands, whose relation as to this, I am bound to believe'; or they might even brazenly state, as Aphra Behn does in one of her fantastical 'true histories': 'I do not pretend to entertain you with a feign'd story, or any thing piec'd together with *Romantick* Accidents; but every Circumstance, to a Tittle, is Truth. To a great part of the Main, I my self was an Eye witness; and what I did not see, I was confirm'd of by Actors in the Intrigue, holy Men, of the Order of St *Francis*.'

Cameras for Tintin, monks for Behn: both are fictional devices set in place to give the fiction itself the veneer of authenticity. Behn, like Tintin, even appears as a character in the thick of the action she purports to relate. The splitting-off of levels of reality that this type of duplicity brings about is brilliantly exploited at the very beginning of the seventeenth century by the less Puritan, more mischievous Miguel de Cervantes, who has his hero spend much of the first volume of *Don Quixote* imagining the style and wording that the written account of his exploits will use. The book's second volume is shown *in* the book, being handed to Quixote himself as a manuscript delivered by a doctor who has found it in a ruined chapel; before the events it contains are relayed to the public, Quixote and a scholar are shown reading and discussing their more salient points.

This type of paradox and playfulness is present in the *Tintin* strips right from the outset. If the *Petit Vingtième's* announcement has, despite its lowbrow, modern context, highly literary, seventeenth-century echoes, this is because its real author Hergé, like Defoe, means the account it prefaces to convey through fictive means a deeper 'truth' – in this case, the reality of Soviet Russia. Three stories later, in *The Cigars of the Pharaoh*, Tintin will be shown sitting in a Bedouin tent being presented, like Quixote, with a manuscript which depicts his own adventures – that is, being handed a *Tintin* book. Here, too, is a splitting-off of levels of reality; only Hergé's reality is split into one more level than even Cervantes' or Behn's, breaking out of the page into reality itself – into the *real* real world. On 8 May 1930, to coincide with the cartoon Tintin's return from Moscow after a year and a half's adventuring, a huge reception was orchestrated at the Gare du Nord in his native Brussels. A blond teenager was tufted up, dressed in Russian clothes and slipped onto the Cologne–Brussels train in Louvain, arriving, as already 'reported' in the newspaper, to be greeted by rapturous crowds – not actors but genuinely delirious young readers. A few weeks later this boy reverted to comic-strip-hero mode to be depicted in the *Petit Vingtième* leaving the same station for Africa, under journalistic contract once again.

As far as its storyline goes, Tintin's first adventure, which after appearing in serial form in *Le Petit Vingtième* was published in 1930 as a freestanding book entitled *Tintin in the Land of the Soviets*, is fairly straightforward. The reporter (who has no particular brief other than to find out what is going on in Russia) is dogged by assassins who try to kill him; he escapes; they come at him again and he escapes again; this pattern is repeated until he makes it home to Brussels. As far as characterisation is concerned, the villains are pantomime cut-outs, and the hero's only attributes are strength, good looks, compassion (he buys a meal for a Bolshevik agent whom he takes to be a beggar and cries when he believes his beloved Snowy has been killed) and moral principles that prompt him to take a stand against injustice even when to do so places him in danger. He also has a sceptical mind, prying behind the surfaces of things to find that what seems to be a fully operating factory is in fact merely a stage set, that what appears to be a haunted house is actually rigged with hidden gramophone and speaker. He is sly, and helps the Kulaks, or bourgeois peasants, hide their grain from the Soviet soldiers in whose search party he has himself enlisted. That is as complicated as it gets. But as Tintin adventure follows Tintin adventure over the following years and decades, a curiously double-edged phenomenon occurs: the straightforward sequences and storylines of the first work mutate into ones which are both infinitely more complex yet still recognisably the same, as we will see. The hero, pitted against ever more morally corrupt antagonists and placed in ever more tangled and ambiguous situations, remains impossibly strong, beautiful, compassionate and principled – in short, impossibly straightforward – while nonetheless retaining his intelligence. Indeed, as we will also see, his scepticism develops into a general world view; his slyness seeps to every level of the texts.

The Tintin books, as we know them now, are stupendously rich. Characters such as Captain Haddock and Bianca Castafiore rival any dreamt up by Dickens or Flaubert for sheer strength and depth of personality. Professor Calculus could hold his own against any number of literary scientists from Marlowe's Doctor Faustus to Brecht's Galileo. The supporting characters, from fiery sub-Guevaran General Alcazar to bitter and twisted multi-millionaire Laszlo Carreidas, billow off the page in all their awkwardness, their childishness, capriciousness. Even the most minor among them exude a presence far beyond that which we might expect from a novelist, let alone a cartoonist: the girthy, thunderous but frightened Americanist Hercules Tarragon of *The Seven Crystal Balls*; the neatly perverted kleptomaniac civil servant Aristides Silk of *The Secret of the Unicorn*; right down to the nameless airport official whose constant fiddling with rubber bands so irritates the Captain in *Tintin in Tibet*. Even the ones we do not meet manage to fill space with their presence: *The Broken Ear*'s murdered sculptor Jacob Balthazar, whose down-at-heel garret speaks volumes of loneliness and semi-realised artistry and whose identity is hollowly reconstituted by his parrot who booms, comically and (for so many reasons) sadly too: 'I am Balthazar!' – or Balthazar's murderer, the cunning thief Rodrigo Tortilla, who cowers in his ship's cabin and whose name his fellow villains mock before they murder him and drop him in the sea.

Like many of the very best writers (Shakespeare and Chaucer spring to mind in this respect), Hergé has bequeathed a bestiary of human types. Taken together, they form a huge social tableau – what Balzac, describing the network of characters spread across his books, calls a *comédie humaine*, a 'human comedy' – made of emirs, barons, butchers whose telephone numbers keep getting confused with one's own and ghastly petit-bourgeois *louches* who are too socially insensitive to realise when neither they nor the insurance they peddle are wanted. You know the type: you might even, in your more honest moments, detect a strain of it in yourself. When these figures are thrown together in the *Tintin* books the tense, loaded situations that arise are managed with all the subtlety normally attributed to Jane Austen or Henry James. People misunderstand one another. Discussions are shown taking place behind the main conversations, in the background, dialogues whose content we can infer from the context (look at Captain Haddock trying to persuade Professor Calculus that he never meant to trick him into thinking they had landed in Botany Bay in *Flight 714*, or Tintin explaining to him that his collar-stud popped when he bent over to kiss Bianca Castafiore's hand in *The Castafiore Emerald*). Exegeses vital to the plot are off-set by, for example, one participant's continuous attempts to prompt another into offering him wine, as in the sequence in Professor Topolino's kitchen in *The Calculus Affair*. Molière-style social comedy runs effortlessly into Dumas-style adventure with Conradian boxed narratives throughout which, thanks to the Captain, volleys of Rabelaisian obscenities echo and boom. A huge symbolic register runs through the books, turning (as we will see) around signs such as the sun, water, the house, even tobacco – a register that, consistent and expanding at the same time, is worthy of a Faulkner or a Brontë. Played out against a backdrop of wars, revolutions and recessions, of technological progress imbued with an almost sacred aspect, not to mention old gods who steadfastly refuse to die, all of this amasses to an *oeuvre* that, again like that of many of the best writers – Stendahl, George Eliot or Pynchon, for example – forms a lens, or prism, through which a whole era lurches into focus.

All of which raises the question: is it literature? Should we, when we read the *Tintin* books, treat them with the reverence we would afford to Shakespeare, Dickens, Rabelais and so on? When we ponder and discuss them, should we bring the same critical apparatus to bear as we would when analysing Flaubert, James or Conrad? In the last two decades of the twentieth century and the first of the twenty-first, writers of cartoons, hugely indebted to Hergé's work, have deliberately launched bids for literary status, producing 'graphic novels' that are often quite self-consciously highbrow and demanding. The huge irony is that the *Tintin* books remain both unrivalled in their complexity and depth *and* so simple, even after more than half a century, that a child can read them with the same involvement as an adult. Adults do read them: there is a wealth of studies, some of which we will encounter over the following pages, assessing Hergé's work from psychoanalytical, political, thematic and technical angles, just as critics might the work of poets, novelists and playwrights. Does it follow that if the same analytical criteria can be applied to one thing as to another, the two things must innately be the same? Or is this bad logic, fit only for cultural theory seminars and Buffy-the-Vampire-Slayer-as-Postmodern-Signifier conferences?

As soon as we ask if *Tintin* should be treated as literature, we raise another question: what is literature? What makes a piece of writing 'literary' rather than journalistic, propagandistic, scientific or so on? This question is a fraught one; you can trace versions of it pretty much all the way back to Plato. In modern times, the thinkers who have best addressed it have tended to be French. In his 1948 essay 'What is Literature?', Jean-Paul Sartre argues that the essence of the literary experience is a kind of freedom linked to a responsibility for others; at the heart of writing, he claims, lies a striving for an autonomous social vision that overcomes alienation, connecting people to the world around them while not being in thrall to any dogma. This fairly sums up the liberal-humanist position on the literary question. For the much more radical Georges Bataille (of whom more later), literature is tied in with evil – not evil understood in any lay sense (the sense in which Hitler or Pol Pot could be described as 'evil') but rather as a tortured and ecstatic rupture of all laws and systems; in works such as his 1957 book *Literature and Evil*, Bataille suggests that at the heart of writing lies a moment of excess and abjection incompatible with liberal values such as liberty and responsibility. For Bataille's friend and accomplice Maurice Blanchot, who spent a whole lifetime pondering the issue in essays such as 'Literature and the Right to Death', literature is linked inextricably with (as the title suggests) death – or at least with a space of dying in which language itself comes to grief, losing its capacity to signify directly.

All of these (and we could look at several more) are working definitions, or at least parameters. You may agree or disagree with them. We could go through the *Tintin* books and find ways in which, according to one or other of the criteria that these definitions and parameters impose, Hergé's work could or could not be considered 'literary'. But I want, for the moment at least, to side-step the question, or rather to approach it from sideways on, via the work of another twentieth-century French thinker, one whose humorous, sensitive and brilliant vision manages to encompass wrestling, Proust, tomato tins, photography and Goethe without ever becoming kitsch, banal or formulaic: Roland Barthes.

Barthes, who was born in 1915 and died beneath the wheels of a laundry van in 1980, dedicated as much time and effort to studying literature as any of his contemporaries. But in the work that made his name, the 1970 book *S/Z*, in which he painstakingly analyses what for him is an exemplary literary text, Honoré de Balzac's 1830 novella *Sarrasine*, he comes at the literary question from the angle not of literary essence but rather of *narrative*. How is a narrative produced? he asks. What gives rise to it, causes it to happen? The answer he quickly comes up with – and here we should revisit our image of Tintin stepping off the station platform to carry out his assignments – is that narrative is born from a contract. Barthes is not just thinking of the contract between publisher and author, but also of one whose terms are established within the text itself, allowing its telling to take place. *Sarrasine* tells the story of a sculptor who falls madly – and fatally – in love with the opera singer la Zambinella. Before Sarrasine dies, he makes a sculpture of her, which is later used by a painter as his model for the Greek god Adonis. The novella itself begins decades after both these events when, at a party given by the fashionable Paris family the de Lantys, the gorgeous young Mme de Rochefide sees the painting and asks her companion (the narrator) to tell her the story behind it. The narrator, in love, or at least lust, with Mme de Rochefide, meets her the next night in 'a small, elegant salon' and, seated on cushions at the foot of the low sofa on which she reclines, starts recounting Sarrasine's tale.

As Barthes points out, Mme de Rochefide wants to know the secret of Adonis; the narrator knows it; the narrator wants her body; and thus 'the conditions for a contract are met'. Indeed, says Barthes, it is this contract rather than Sarrasine's doomed love for la Zambinella that is the novella's primary story. The story of Sarrasine himself is 'legal tender . . . economic stakes, in short, *merchandise*, barter' – and its recounting raises a question we should ask of every narrative: what is it 'worth'? What should it be exchanged for? If *Sarrasine* is an exemplary literary text, it is because the dramatising of this question forms its action.

Barthes's insight, I would argue, opens up a seam that runs right to the heart of Hergé's work. The *Tintin* books, which originated in a newspaper's desire to increase circulation by recruiting younger readers, show, again and again, narrative

turned into merchandise, subjected to barter. Tintin goes to
Russia under contract, and the 'photographs' he supposedly
himself sends back to honour that contract form the content
of the work. He goes to Africa for the same reasons. No
sooner does he arrive there in the second Tintin adventure,
Tintin au Congo, than representatives of rival newspapers
swoop on him to bid for his story. This type of bartering for
narrative takes place in many other fields than simply journalism. In *The Secret of the Unicorn* we see an antiques dealer's
man bid for the model ship Tintin has just bought in a flea
market, desperate to obtain the parchment lodged inside its
mast, key to another story (that of where the seventeenth-century naval commander Sir Francis Haddock buried treasure
he plundered from another plunderer, Red Rackham). In
The Broken Ear Tintin and a villainous duo bid against one
another for a parrot who has witnessed a murder, both hoping
to cajole it into repeating the fatal scene's dialogue – that is,
into narrating. The old gypsy woman in *The Castafiore
Emerald* cajoles the other way, urging Haddock to pay her to
tell his fortune. When Haddock refuses she grabs his palm
and exclaims, 'Oooooh!', and Haddock gasps: 'What is it? . . .
Tell me!' Good sellers know all the tricks, the peddler's patter.
Take Oliveira da Figueira, the Lisbon trader who sells stories
like he sells prams and bars of soap: the fabulous yarn he
spins Müller's servants in *Land of Black Gold*, a tale of snail
farmers, pirates and counts, is told strategically to keep the
servants busy while Tintin sneaks into Müller's castle.
Sarrasine's story is also told strategically, by a man who hopes
it will help him sneak into a woman's knickers. Pointing out

that it, too, is 'perhaps fictitious, in the fiction itself: counterfeit money surreptitiously put in circulation', Barthes compares it to the tales told by possibly the most famous and certainly the most strategic storyteller of all, *The Thousand and One Nights'* Scheherazade, whose stories are exchanged against her life: if she stops narrating, she will be beheaded.

What is the status of a narrative? Of the text that carries it? And what do these put at stake? In *The Cigars of the Pharaoh* a travel brochure is confused with a papyrus indicating the whereabouts of the lost tomb of Kih-Oskh. This confusion overtakes Tintin, who sets out on a cruise but ends up locked in a pyramid. In both this album and the next, *The Blue Lotus*, we have instances of the switched letter trick first used by Shakespeare's Hamlet on his guardians Rosencrantz and Guildenstern. The first switch places Tintin in an asylum (unbeknown to him, the substituting letter states – and here more parallels with *Hamlet* could be made – that he is mad); the second frees him and loses those latter-day Rosencrantz and Guildenstern, Thompson and Thomson, their catch (unbeknown to them, the substituting letter states that *they* are mad). In *Land of Black Gold* fake documents implicate Tintin in an entirely fictitious arms-smuggling plot, nearly costing him his life; in *Tintin and the Picaros* Sponsz's forged papers ensnare and almost kill Tintin's whole entourage.

In the *Tintin* books, narratives are bought and sold, stolen and substituted, or twisted out of shape until, turned inside out or back to front, they mutate into other narratives – even when no one is trying. Look at the overlap of stories in the garden sequence of *The Castafiore Emerald*. The journalists think they are on to a sensational discovery about the nature of the relationship between Captain Haddock and Bianca Castafiore. They ask Professor Calculus when the marriage will take place, where the couple met and so on. The hard-of-hearing professor thinks that they are asking him about the new variety of rose he is developing, and explains to them that it all depends on the weather, it began at the Chelsea Flower Show and so forth. They file a feature telling of the forthcoming wedding and the lovers' meeting at the Chelsea Flower Show. 'We must be sure,' the diligent photographer says, to which the much more savvy writer answers: 'True or not, Marco my boy, it'll sell!' The printed story that mutates like some hybrid monster out of other stories' parts is, as Barthes would say, 'counterfeit money put in circulation'. Captain Haddock's civil status as a bachelor is at stake in it; but what it brings him is not marriage but a flood of telegrams and letters – a flood, that is, of other texts.

Tenez-nous bien au courant, the avuncular editor-figure tells Tintin as he boards the train for Moscow: 'Keep us posted.' In his hotel room, Tintin writes reams of copy: pages that pile up and fall onto the floor but never get sent. What we are seeing, right at the outset of the *Tintin oeuvre*, is a drama about the appearance and circulation of stories – also about their disappearance and re-emergence in another form. This drama continues, growing more and more sophisticated as the books progress. As with *Sarrasine*, stories become embedded within other stories. They also become embedded within animals and objects. Behind *The Broken Ear*'s fetish or *The Secret of the Unicorn*'s ship, there is a story – a story that has value because it leads to a diamond, to diamonds, to wealth. Object, narrative, object: a loop. Text and object merge into one another: inside the hollowed-out mast of the model *Unicorn* lies a parchment. Conversely, in *Explorers on the Moon* a bottle of whisky is hidden inside the Captain's fake *Guide to Astronomy*: the text, in this case, is hollow, smuggling something else.

'Isn't that a fine ship!' says Tintin when he sees the model *Unicorn* in the flea market. 'It's a unique specimen,' the stallholder tells him. 'It's a very old . . . er . . . very old type of galliard.' Clearly, neither of them is aware of what the ship contains. The scene is allegorical. What it wants to tell us is this: when narrative is subjected to a barter economy, the terms are not fixed. You never know quite what you are selling or what you are buying. You might end up with more than you bargained for, or you might simply have been had.

ii

The *Tintin* books announce themselves on their front covers as 'Adventures'. This, plus their action-packed nature, might suggest that they are dominated by what Barthes, in S/Z, calls the 'proairetic code' – that is, the code of action. But in fact another code is equally, if not more, dominant: the code

Barthes calls the 'hermeneutic'. What does the hermeneutic do? It is made up, Barthes tells us, of all the aspects of a text that 'constitute an enigma and lead to its solution'.

Tintin's adventures are framed by enigmas: from the social enigma of the Soviet Union to the scientific enigma of the shooting star to the supernatural enigma of the Sun God's curse. Tintin is caught up in these and ends up solving them. No wonder he is often mistakenly referred to as a 'detective'. The books display an after-the-crime logic, poring over the scene of events that happened either recently (a drowned sailor and a kidnapped Japanese man in *The Crab with the Golden Claws*) or in a previous century (the shipwreck in *Red Rackham's Treasure*). In *The Broken Ear* we get both: the theft of a fetish from the Museum of Ethnography in the mid-twentieth century and the earlier theft, in the late nineteenth, of a diamond from the Arumbaya tribe – two embedded narratives running alongside one another, or rather sedimented layers of the same one, staggered back. As the book advances, Tintin moves backwards through time, looping back to catch up with the anthropologist A. J. Walker's book *Travels in the Americas* which he reads at *The Broken Ear's* beginning, going to the earlier text's source. In *Red Rackham's Treasure* he goes to the source of the seventeenth-century naval commander Sir Francis Haddock's diaries, which the Captain (Sir Francis's descendant) has read and recounted to him in *The Secret of the Unicorn*. It is as though he were in the sway of a massively retroactive compulsion – what the nineteenth-century writer Charles Baudelaire calls 'always concerned with looking for noon at two o'clock'.

Enigma-solving is never straightforward. Hermeneutic sequences are full of what Barthes describes as 'reticence'. The narrative sets up obstacles: delays, snares, partial or suspended answers and straightforward 'jamming'. This is everywhere in *Tintin*. In *The Secret of the Unicorn* the man who comes to spill the beans about what is happening to Tintin and Haddock is shot; the information he manages to give them before passing out (pointing at birds to designate the Bird Brothers as his assailants) is 'good' but incomprehensible: 'Sparrows?' Tintin asks. The wallet containing one of the three parchments needed to discover the location of the treasure is stolen; even when the parchments are assembled they are unreadable, a jumble of fragmented numbers. In *The Blue Lotus* two messengers who come to brief Tintin are poisoned and made mad; the villain Mitsuhirato, posing as his friend, gives him bad information; the über-villain Rastapopoulos, also posing as his friend, gives him correct but misleading information.

Villains and situations misdirect the characters, and Hergé misdirects the reader. In both *The Cigars of the Pharaoh* and *The Blue Lotus* he slyly cuts between scenes of villains writing and reading dispatches and Thompson and Thomson sending reports and receiving orders, deceptively implying that the two go together. He delights in 'doubling'. Two separate people vie with Tintin for the ship in *The Secret of the Unicorn*; when it is stolen we wrongly assume, like Tintin, that the more insistent one has stolen it. Two agents from competing foreign powers spy on the occupants of Haddock's ancestral home Marlinspike in *The Calculus Affair*; when the Professor returns to the house with a bullet-hole in his hat, we suppose that one of them has shot at him, before realising that his hat was merely the recipient of a stray bullet fired by one rival agent at the other.

This doubling is played out at a smaller-than-plot level too. The books abound in what we might call 'double-articulation': a clap of thunder followed immediately by the CLING of broken windows in *The Calculus Affair* (we will at first assume the two are linked); two bangs which sound like gunshots but turn out to be car tyres exploding followed by a bang caused by a shutter slamming in *The Seven Crystal Balls* (these are themselves followed by a clap of thunder; by the next morning a gun will have been fired). The effect of this double-articulation is to mislead, send sideways, lull, jolt, skid, pull back.

To solve a mystery you need to work stuff out – and obviously, this involves acts of interpretation. What Barthes's talk of the 'hermeneutic' aspects of a text should show us, beyond the fact that most stories have at least a slight detective element to them, is that the activity of reading does not begin only after the writing stops. On the contrary, most interesting texts *already* contain moments of reading, acts of interpretation. The *Tintin* books are full of them. Tintin reads books, parchments, scraps of crab-tin label, coded puzzles. Landscape itself is legible, via tyre- and footprints left in earth and snow, names scrawled on rocks. As the psychoanalyst Serge Tisseron points out in his 1990 study *Tintin et les Secrets de Famille* (*Tintin and Family Secrets*), objects in cartoons are 'made present in their most active figural capacity'. Mixing images and words, the medium can turn things into language and language into a thing – a process that is played out self-consciously via huge letter-blocks in the unfinished *Tintin and Alph-Art*. While Tintin reads, others misread. In *Prisoners of the Sun* Calculus interprets the Inca ceremony as a film-shoot, while Thompson and Thomson, carrying a pendulum and dowsing manual in an effort to locate their friends, hope-lessly 'convert' the signals they receive from these into the world around them, visiting a mine when the pendulum (cor-rectly) indicates that Captain Haddock is depressed or 'low'.

Interpretation, misinterpretation: considered from this angle, Tintin is the *oeuvre*'s hero not because he is the strongest or most principled or compassionate, but because he is the best reader. He manages to decode the puzzle whose torn-up pieces he finds in the buried jackets of the crashed, unmarked plane's pilots in *The Black Island*, realising that '3 f.r. Δ' designates the three red flares, laid out in a triangle, with whose aid the pilots' accomplices on the ground signal to them where to drop the sacks of counterfeit money they are transporting. He works out, in a stroke of three-dimensional genius, that the parchments in *The Secret of the Unicorn* will only reveal their message when they are superimposed and held up to the light: by overlaying three texts, reading *through* them, he unearths meaning that any one of the three is inca-pable of expressing on its own. He reads *across* as well: from object to name, as when he eventually realises that the birds at which the same book's shot bean-spiller was pointing actually designate two men named Bird; and from name to event, as when he deduces from the title of Puccini's opera *La Gazza*

Ladra – 'The Thieving Magpie' – that the real thief in *The Castafiore Emerald* is neither gypsy, monkey, maid, butler nor pianist but (again) a bird. In short, he can navigate the world of signs.

Of course, he never gets there straight away. Over the course of each book he experiences what James Joyce in his 1939 novel *Finnegans Wake* calls 'corrective unrest' – that is, a general need to keep making corrections. After tracking the villains of *The Broken Ear* via their car number plate to an address only to find two old men who bear no resemblance to Alonso Perez and Ramón Bada, he reasons that the bystander who relayed the numbers cannot have seen them clearly, then that Perez and Bada might have used false plates – before dropping his notebook and viewing it from upside down, whereupon the sequence 169MW flips over to correctly read MW691. After fruitlessly searching the ocean for the island described by Sir Francis Haddock in his diaries, he realises in *Red Rackham's Treasure* that he and Captain Haddock have been using the Greenwich Meridian to calculate degrees of longitude, whereas the seventeenth-century Sir Francis would have used the Paris one. Later, in a moment of inspiration worthy of the Argentinean writer Jorge Luis Borges (who also, incidentally, invented a pirate called Rackham), he corrects from world to map, and finds the treasure hidden not at the bottom of the ocean but in the globe in Marlinspike. Thompson and Thomson, meanwhile, make bad corrections, telling Captain Haddock that 'there really is a little mistake in your calculations. Look, this is where we are, exactly . . .' The Captain removes his hat and prays, recognising the coordinates they have come up with as those of Westminster Abbey. He may mock them, but he is not above making bad corrections himself: in *The Calculus Affair* he 'corrects' his initial understanding that lightning caused his glass and vases to break into an accusation that it was Snowy – wide of the mark both times, since it was neither of these but rather Calculus's ultra-sonic weapon.

As the characters correct, so do the readers. The 'gunshots' of *The Seven Crystal Balls* are 'corrected' to tyres (as though that could arrest the chain of semi-repetitions); the parachutists captured in the forbidden zone around the factory in *Destination Moon* are 'corrected' into Thompson and Thomson; the phone in *The Castafiore Emerald* is 'corrected' into the parrot who has learnt to imitate its ring, then, as soon as we begin assuming that the sound comes from the parrot, back into the phone. 'Aim a little to the left'; 'more to the right'; 'more to the west'; 'Caramba! Missed again!' How do we, as readers, know when we have got it right, if our corrections are good ones? What would our 'treasure' be? Some kind of consistency, the story making sense? Or does this simply lull us, divert our gaze so that something else can be smuggled aboard?

The desert of *Land of Black Gold* is a space of multiple misreadings. Mirages, hollow signs of the heat-glow, are taken for objects and people; objects and people are taken for mirages. Tintin, who thanks to those fake documents has been taken for someone else, witnesses an air drop in which scores of government propaganda leaflets rain down on Bab

El Ehr's rebels. 'None of my men can read!' the sheikh roars with laughter – before a heavy, tied-up stack of leaflets lands right on his head. Soon, Tintin is abandoned in the desert without water. Thompson and Thomson, looking for him in a jeep, inadvertently drive in a large loop and, coming across the tracks they themselves made an hour ago, take these for the tracks of another car, which they decide to follow. An hour later they of course loop back and, finding the inter-section they made earlier, exclaim: 'More tracks! ... A second car joined the first one.' As the hours go by they rejoin their own tracks again and again, believing each time that the highway they are following has grown busier and busier. This brilliantly allegorical scene is endlessly regress-ive: what Thompson and Thomson are doing is failing to recognise that they are not only reading their own mark but also reading their own reading of their mark, their interpre-tation of their own interpretation. Tintin, crouching over the tracks, realises what is going on but has no means of com-municating. Then the Khamsin whips itself into action: a ferocious sandstorm that soon wipes all tracks away. An orgy of marking, reading and misreading, followed by total era-sure, total inscrutability. As Tintin huddles, despondent, endless grains of sand hit his eyes and mouth, like so many illegible tracts.

iii

During the Khamsin, the desert's visual field dissolves into orphaned sounds and disembodied voices: Tintin hears Thompson and Thomson's motor, shouts out, fires his gun. The detectives think they are hearing a 'sound mirage'. They are wrong, of course – but not *that* wrong: the *Tintin* books are full of acts of sound projection, of ventriloquism. Thompson and Thomson themselves ventriloquise the voice of the god Siva from behind his altar in *The Cigars of the Pharaoh*, scaring away the Indians who are about to sacrifice Snowy, just as the explorer Ridgewell ventriloquises that of the Rumbaba spirits in *The Broken Ear*, tricking the South American tribe into sparing him and Tintin from sacrifice. Parrots ventriloquise throughout the *oeuvre*, as do gramophones and cassette players. In *The Castafiore Emerald*, Marlinspike Hall is awash with sounds that have been cut off from their source and replicated, like echoes in mountains: piano scales, a telephone's ring-tone, thuds, cries of 'Mercy my jewels!' . . .

In S/Z Barthes describes literature as a 'stereographic space' in which utterances are 'de-originated'; in its 'dissolve of voices' the question 'Who speaks?' is never properly answered. The text, he writes, 'stages a certain "noise"' whose 'various listeners (here we ought to be able to say *écouteur* as we say *voyeur*) seem to be located at every corner of the utterance, each waiting for an origin he reverses with a second gesture into the flux of the reading'. 'Hello-o-o! I can hear you!' coos the parrot, echoing Castafiore, posing as Captain Haddock. Think of all the instances of eavesdropping we get throughout the books: Nestor listening at the door to Tintin and the Captain arguing in *Tintin and the Picaros*; Tintin listening from inside a vase to Mitsuhirato issuing instructions to his hoods in *The Blue Lotus*; Bab El Ehr's spy listening as Tintin and the Emir hatch their plan in *The Red Sea Sharks* – there are many more. In *King Ottokar's Sceptre* there is even a double-eavesdropping as Tintin stands in a hallway listening in on the gang listening in on Alembick.

The casting and consuming of voices are sometimes done by mouths and ears alone, but mostly they are done through technology. Written in the century when communication technology erupted and transformed the world forever, the *Tintin* books come back repeatedly to moments of *transmission*. Forget journalism: what Tintin actually *does* is send and receive radio messages. This is his job on the boat in *Land of Black Gold* and in the rocket of *Explorers on the Moon*. Some of Hergé's most striking images are not of characters or actions but of radio masts, wires casting signals and antennae picking them up. In both *Cigars of the Pharaoh* and *The Red Sea Sharks* Tintin floats on the ocean while radio transmissions billow and swirl around him. In *The Blue Lotus* he tracks a radio transmitter to its source: this is the book's plot in a nutshell. In this respect he resembles Caliban in Shakespeare's *The Tempest*, who describes the air around him as 'full of noises, sounds and sweet airs'; or the same play's Ferdinand who, picking up Ariel's transmissions, wonders: 'Where should this music be? In the air or the earth? . . . I have followed it/ or it hath drawn me rather . . .' Most of all he resembles the eponymous hero of Jean Cocteau's 1950 film *Orphée*, who sweeps through the spectrum as he manically fiddles with the dial. 'WHEET . . . CRACK . . . CRR . . . dernières nouvelles d'Europe . . . CRR . . . ДA? . . . ДA? . . . HNET! . . . HNET! . . . CRR. . . . The European news service . . .' crackles Oliveira da Figueira's radio as Tintin tunes it in *Land of Black Gold*. 'BEEP-BEEP-BEEP . . . 724 . . . 326 . . . Listen: the bird sings with its fingers . . . Two times . . . BEEP-BEEP . . .' crackles Cocteau's in *Orphée*. When asked why he is listening to it, Orphée responds: 'I'm tracking the unknown.'

Hergé's transmission zones are also hermeneutic zones, full of enigmas which need solving. 'What can it possibly mean?' Tintin asks as he picks up Mitsuhirato's cryptic wireless messages in *The Blue Lotus*. Here, too, is reticence; here, too, are snares and misleading signals. Here, too, is corrective unrest. 'No, Madam, this is not Marlinspike 431. This is 421, Madam.' 'Correction: three, two, seven, six . . . Repeat . . .' 'Three, two, seven, six . . . Correction made'; 'Correction: seven, eight, five, two. Correct it, this time!' Another allegorical episode: these partial corrections, made to the radio-guidance system of Calculus's trial rocket in *Destination Moon*, are doomed. They will never hold because the signal has been intercepted, the frequency hijacked.

For the second volume of *Hermès*, the grand study of communication he conducted through the 1970s and '80s, the philosopher (and friend of Hergé) Michel Serres chose the title *Interference*. He dedicates a whole chapter of it to *The Castafiore Emerald*. The real subject of this book, he tells us, is the communication network itself – and this is 'stuffed with untruths, misdirections, imbecilities, pure noise'. Seeing local monitor images of the interview being recorded with Bianca Castafiore in the next room, Professor Calculus mistakes transmission for reception and rushes in to tell her that she is on television. 'Receptions, interceptions,' Serres writes: some interceptions break the message; others go in and grab it, like the photographer from the Italian magazine *Tempo di Roma* who goes in and snaps illicit photos. He, perhaps, is the *real* thief, just as the message's *real* transmitter is perhaps hiding a couple of links down the chain. In another sense, the communication network robs itself: 'Multiply the detours, mediations and codes,' Serres warns, 'and you lose the treasure along the way. Who steals it? The pie, of course, the chatterbox – that is, the excess of language itself.' This type of excess, misdirection and scrambling happens throughout the *Tintin* books to transmissions of all kinds: deliberately, accidentally, through technological error or accidents of geography or nature. '. . . ry . . . cet . . . ing . . . wo . . . ump . . . ca . . .' 'What? . . . What? . . . Shout louder! The wind's too strong! . . . I can't hear you!' 'Hello? . . . *FRRWT* . . . Hello, I can't hear you *CLACK* . . . What? . . . *FRRT* . . . *CRRACK* . . . Can't you speak up!' 'What a line!' It is no coincidence that Calculus, the man of knowledge, himself has a broken ear.

Amidst all this cacophony, these signals sent in all directions, Hergé's work keeps pointing towards another audio space, a dead zone off the sonar, one whose signals manage to elude detection. This zone is where the *real* action takes place. Rastapopoulos's area of activity in *Flight 714* lies beneath the radar field, just as *The Black Island*'s forgers broadcast on a frequency the police cannot track down. As Tintin finds out in *The Calculus Affair*, it is the transmissions you cannot hear that are the loaded, dangerous ones. The information Calculus most wants his trial rocket to obtain in *Destination Moon* lies in the radio blind spot on the moon's far side. The horizon, disappearance, absolute erasure: this, perhaps, is where the *Tintin* books are ultimately oriented, their magnetic north. Their tendency to turn towards blind spots of all sorts, move into dead zones in all senses of the word, trawl over horizons both spatial and symbolic, is played out in many ways, as we will see. And we will also see, perhaps, that, taken as a whole, Hergé's work, like Balzac's, has what Barthes calls a 'vanishing point', a spot in which it 'seems to be keeping in reserve some ultimate meaning, one it does not express'. It could be that this spot holds the ultimate truth of the *Tintin* books, their secret. Or it could equally turn out that this spot lies at what Barthes calls 'the degree zero of meaning'; that what it holds in store is not the treasure of the unexpressed but, borrowing Barthes's words again, 'the signifier of the inexpressible'.

iv

Hergé let illustration be invaded by the avant-garde. In the very first *Tintin* book he makes a knowing reference to the iconoclastic painter Kasimir Malevich by presenting (after Tintin throws the light switch as he runs from his assassins) a panel of black on black: marking to the point of erasure. The books are full of erasure: dematriculated planes; wiped runways; wiped memories; a ship whose name (*Karaboudjan*) has been removed and replaced; a city whose name (Los Dopicos) is removed, replaced, removed and replaced again. The books are both full of erasure and subject to it themselves: as Hergé transferred the stories from their original newspaper and then magazine versions to the album format in which we now read them, he reworked them, covering up material he considered out of date or below par. Like the Khamsin he wiped out old marks, but like Thompson and Thomson he picked them up too, reprising previous sequences and patterns (the detectives again follow their tracks in a circle on the moon), embedding former stories (the plots of the two previous books appear as current-affairs items on the television programme 'Scanorama' in *The Castafiore Emerald*), repeating and developing the same themes (hidden wealth, succession and usurpation, copying or duplication and rituals of hospitality, to name but a few) again and again.

Nor does it stop there. Hergé was subject to erasure himself. His very name, or rather *nom de plume*, was born from a double-move of covering up and rewriting: taking the initials of his real name Georges Remi, he reversed them into *RG* or, written as this is pronounced in French, *Hergé*. In using this word as his signature, he hid even as he made himself most public. Like Hitchcock, he occasionally slipped himself into his images – but meekly, concealing himself in crowds. He started out with low regard for what he did, not considering it proper art (he lasted just one day at art school). Later, emboldened by a critic's description of him as the *Roi-Soleil* or 'Sun King' of the comic format, he attempted 'proper' painting and showed the results to the curator of the Musées Royaux de Beaux-Arts in Brussels. A huge *Tintin* fan, the curator told him they were rubbish. Later still, encouraged by the incorporation of cartoons into the work of modernist painters such as Robert Rauschenberg and Roy Lichtenstein (whose work Hergé collected), he visited Andy Warhol and asked him if he thought *Tintin* was pop-art too. Warhol merely stared back, smiling inanely. Hergé's final, incomplete book *Tintin and Alph-Art*, which we will look at in more detail later, betrays in its massive self-reflexiveness a desire to be taken seriously, to be seen to be considering the highly conceptual issues in contemporary art with which its author is clearly *au fait*, alongside a desire to mock the highness of the establishment that never accepted him as highbrow, to expose its pretentiousness, its fraudulence.

And literature? Hergé grew up reading lowbrow books. Later in life he read Proust and Balzac. He even read Barthes. But he never aspired to be considered a 'writer'. And here we loop back, like Thompson and Thomson, to the curving track we laid down earlier, and rejoin the question: should we now claim, posthumously, on Hergé's behalf, that in fact he *was* a writer, and a great one? My short answer to this question is: no. My longer answer is that the claim we should make for him is a more interesting one. And it revolves around two paradoxes. The first, as I suggested earlier, is that wrapped up in a simple medium for children is a mastery of plot and symbol, theme and sub-text far superior to that displayed by most 'real' novelists. If you want to be a writer, study *The Castafiore Emerald,* and study it carefully. It holds all literature's formal keys, its trade secrets – and holds them at the vanishing point of plot, where nothing whatsoever happens.

To confuse comics with literature would be a mistake, and even more so with the groundbreaking work of Hergé, in which, as Numa Sadoul points out in *Entretiens avec Hergé* (*Encounters with Hergé*), the set of interviews he conducted with Tintin's creator in the mid-seventies, the medium 'takes up an original and autonomous ground between drawing and writing'. Packed with significance, intensely associative, overwhelmingly suggestive, it still occupies a space below the radar of literature proper. Which leads us to the second paradox: this below-radar altitude, this blind spot, this mute pocket is, as we already know, the zone where the real action takes place. Let's call it a degree-zero zone, a kind of loaded anti-space held in reserve. If literature itself has an ultimate truth, a deeper-than-trade secret either unexpressed or inexpressible, it is in precisely this kind of space that we should look for it.

Tintin means, literally, 'Nothing'. His face, round as an *O* with two pinpricks for eyes, is what Hergé himself described as 'the degree zero of typeage' – a typographic vanishing point. Tintin is also the degree zero of personage. He has no past, no sexual identity, no complexities. Like Cocteau's Orphée, who spends much of the film in the negative space or dead world on the far side of the mirror, he is a writer who does not write. As Tintin could tell you, if there are secret operations going on in this degree-zero zone of writing, then these can only be approached by overlaying, reading across, reading through. That is what we will be doing in this book. As we do so we should arm ourselves with Tintin's intuition that while some texts (like the pilots' puzzle), complete on their own, can simply be decoded so as to point to information hidden in the world, others (like each of the three parchments) need supplementing before meaning starts emerging, while others still will generate layers of meaning never intended in the first place when they are connected via some link, however spurious, to another scene, another context that might have emerged quite independently of them (did Puccini intend to tell Tintin where Castafiore's emerald was hidden? Of course not). And we should also be forewarned that, even when we manage to gather all the texts, scenes and contexts together and hold them up for inspection, their real content may still remain invisible, hiding in the light.

2

THEY'RE PINING FOR YOU IN BORDURIA: FASCISM AND FRIENDSHIP

UNE GUERRE DU PÉTROLE (Extrait de « *Isvestia* »)

From *Le Crapouillot*, 1920.

i

Tintin's political origins lie on the right, to put it mildly. The *Petit Vingtième* was a strict Catholic newspaper and, as Hergé himself tells Numa Sadoul, '"Catholic" at that time meant "anti-Bolchevik".' It also meant anti-Semitic. The paper's editor, the Abbé Norbert Wallez, kept a signed photograph of Mussolini on his desk. Many of the journalists who wrote for him had links to the more-or-less fascist Belgian party Rex.

This political orientation not only found its way into the strips; it was their *raison d'être*. Tintin's first outing is primarily a piece of propaganda, 'exposing' the evils of communism. His second, to the Congo (which appeared in book form in French in 1931 but has never been deemed acceptable for translation into English – although, much to the exasperation of European liberals, it remains hugely popular in Africa), depicts Africans as good at heart but backwards and lazy, in need of European mastery. In *The Cigars of the Pharaoh* and *The Blue Lotus*, both of which appeared in the mid-thirties, we have villains who are typical enemies of the right, key players in the great global conspiracy of its imagination: Freemasons, financiers and, behind it all, thinly veiled by a

Greek name, the blatantly Semitic Rastapopoulos. The right-wing strain in Hergé's work reaches its apex when, writing the original newspaper version of *The Shooting Star* at the height of the Nazi era, he invents a Jewish villain (the New York banker Blumenstein) and has a shopkeeper named Isaac rub his hands with glee when it seems the world will end. Why? Because, as he explains to his friend Solomon, 'I owe 50,000 francs to my suppliers, and this way I won't have to pay them.'

But almost as soon as this right-wing tendency gets going it becomes shadowed by a left-wing counter-tendency. In *Tintin in America*, which he published in book form in 1932, Hergé bitingly satirises capitalist mass-production and American racism (the English translation has been softened: what the small-town bank clerk really tells the police who turn up after a heist is: 'We immediately lynched seven negroes' – not 'fellers' – 'but the culprit got away'). In *The Blue Lotus* Tintin snaps the cane with which an American oil magnate has been beating a Chinese rickshaw driver, exclaiming: 'Brute! Your conduct is disgraceful, Sir!' *The Broken Ear*, also from the mid-thirties, contains sequences which, lambasting the greed of multinationals and the cynicism of arms traders, are taken straight from the leftist magazine *Le Crapouillot*, whose March 1932 issue has a profile of the weapons dealer Sir Basil Zaharrof (or, as Hergé renames him, Bazarov) and whose February 1934 number exposes the corporate puppeteers behind the recent Bolivia–Paraguay war over the Gran Chaco (or, as Hergé renames them, 'Gran Chapo') oil fields. While right and left coexist for a while, it would seem that over time the latter wins out over the former – so much so that by the mid-seventies, in *Tintin and the Picaros*, the hero sports a CND sign on his moped helmet.

How is this shift managed? Through a complex set of erasures and re-markings that carried Hergé and his work through the personal and global Khamsin that lay at the heart of his era: World War Two.

When Germany invaded his native Belgium in May 1940, Hergé, who had already done a stint as a reservist the previous year, presented himself for military duty but was rejected on medical grounds. He then took off for Paris. But when, after the general surrender, King Leopold III issued a call to his countrymen to stay and muddle through the occupation, he returned. The *Vingtième Siècle*, like many Belgian newspapers, ceased publication: Wallez may have been fascist but he had also taken issue with Hitler's pagan leanings. Some papers kept going, albeit in what was known as 'stolen' form, under Nazi management. Hordes of journalists resigned rather than collaborate. Hergé went the other way, and in October 1940 started publishing *Tintin* in the stolen *Le Soir*, where it appeared alongside general Nazi propaganda and a couple of anti-Semitic essays by a young man who in future years would become famous as the brilliant critic Paul de Man, of whom more later.

Hergé justified his actions, even years on, with the 'tram conductor' argument. As he reasons with Sadoul in *Entretiens*, if a ticket collector or a baker do their jobs, why should he not? 'But while everyone found it normal that a train driver drives a train,' he complains, 'journalists were branded "traitors"!' The argument may seem stunningly naïve, largely because it is stunningly naïve: a train driver or baker do not actively help control minds and propagate race hatred. But it is interesting inasmuch as it contains a vital proposition: that the artist is a craftsman or technician pure and simple – a proposition that Hergé would play out post-war through the figure of Calculus.

It is also interesting because it marks a move towards *de-politicising* a set of works in which politics had previously played a central role. *Tintin in the Land of the Soviets* and *The Blue Lotus* are, or at least contain, direct satires of actual political situations (Soviet totalitarianism and the Japanese invasion of Manchuria respectively). But as the books move into the war Hergé erases their political specificity. He does this firstly by turning it into fictional allegory: the near-annexation of Syldavia by Borduria in *King Ottokar's Sceptre* (which appeared in *Le Petit Vingtième* in 1938 and in book form in 1939) reflects, but does not directly represent, the German–Austrian *Anschluss*. Then, in *The Shooting Star* (which Hergé started working on in 1941), he turns it into ostensibly non-political metaphor: the stifling atmosphere of the oppressed city does not *explicitly* denote the occupation any more than the name initially given by the astronomer Decimus Phostle to the spider which, magnified by his telescope, appears to be hurtling towards Europe like some horrific catastrophe, *Aranea Fasciata* (lost in the English translation), *explicitly* denotes Nazism – but the insinuations are not hard to pick up. Eventually, though, he removes it completely: politics are entirely absent from the next four books, the double-book adventure *The Secret of the Unicorn* and *Red Rackham's*

Treasure (which Hergé started serialising in *Le Soir* in 1942) and the similarly spread-out *The Seven Crystal Balls* and *Prisoners of the Sun* (which began appearing in 1943).

As his biographer Pierre Assouline points out, the work Hergé produced during the war shows him at the height of his powers as a storyteller and illustrator, and highlights the uncomfortable fact that, creatively speaking, the occupation was a kind of 'golden age' for him. The trauma came at the war's end, with the liberation. As collaborators were rounded up, Hergé, who was halfway through the Peruvian diptych, was arrested and released four times: joined-up administration was slow in arriving to post-liberation Brussels. He avoided trial because the Public Prosecutor felt he would have covered himself in ridicule had he put Tintin in the dock ('Would I have had to subpoena his dog as well?' he asked when challenged on this issue). But Hergé found his name included in a list of '*inciviles*', former collaborators barred from public life. In short, he became *persona non grata* in his own country. Deeply depressed, he thought of emigrating to Argentina, but was rescued, ironically enough, by former *Résistance* hero Raymond Leblanc, who in 1946 founded a bi-weekly magazine named simply *Tintin*, installing Hergé as artistic director and lead author.

Hergé took up where he had left off, finishing *Prisoners of the Sun* and then picking up *Land of Black Gold* where he had abandoned it with the invasion – with the German villain Müller about to put a bullet through Tintin's head. The story begins with war looming, and Hergé uses the second half of it as a kind of wishful retroactive wiping-out of history:

Tintin rumbles Müller's operation and war is averted. In the next two books, *Destination Moon* (published in 1953) and *Explorers on the Moon* (which came out one year later), Professor Calculus embodies Hergé's understanding, or at least interpretation, of his own wartime position, spun out into a post-war environment. How? By figuring as a genius working almost coincidentally within national, political or military frameworks: what really drives him is his work, which quite literally transcends contingencies like these – even if it carries on board, in the anguished character of the engineer Frank Wolff (who, blackmailed by a rival power, hands over secrets and smuggles a deadly stowaway onto the moon rocket), the spectre of betrayal and inexpungeable guilt. Scarcely is the space adventure over than Calculus is whisked off, in *The Calculus Affair* (which Hergé began working on in 1954), to play out the counter-position to, or flip-side of, the one he represented in the moon books: that of genius compromised. Having made 'a sensational discovery in the field of ultrasonics', inventing a sound-device capable of destroying objects from a distance, he is kidnapped by the Bordurian state apparatus, which wants to turn his discovery to war-like ends.

Effectively, Hergé uses Calculus over these three books in a similar way to that in which Thomas Pynchon uses the scientist Franz Pökler in his 1973 novel *Gravity's Rainbow*. Pökler, like Calculus, works at a rocket base. He plays down the political background against which his creative energies are being deployed (that of the war), arguing that soon 'Borders won't mean anything. We'll have all outer space . . .' In the meantime he helps develop the V2 rocket bomb, built by slave labour and masterminded by the same Werner von Braun who in reality, after the Americans and Russians had played a Borduro-Syldavian game of snatch and counter-snatch with him, ended up putting the Apollo mission on the moon. Hergé beat Braun to it (by fifteen years, no less) but relied heavily on his work, as witnessed by the textbook Tintin and Haddock find in Topolino's house, *German Research in World War II* – a real book almost certainly used by Pynchon as a source for *Gravity's Rainbow* (it even has a V2 on its cover). But whereas Pynchon's Pökler ends up coming face-to-face with what his naïvety has suppressed, visiting a concentration camp and realising that he has used his engineering skill as a 'gift of Daedalus that allowed him to put as much labyrinth as required between himself and the inconveniences of caring', Hergé, who refused to believe in the reality of the camps for years, lets Calculus (and, by extension, himself) off much more lightly. At the end of *The Calculus Affair* the Professor is saved by Tintin from either having to help synthesise an ultrasonic bomb or – much closer to Hergé's actual concerns given the atmosphere of trials and confessions in post-war Belgium – being released through juridical process having signed a forced declaration.

Calculus does little more than turn round and round in circles when pushed by Abdullah on his roller-skates in the next book, *The Red Sea Sharks*, which was started in 1956. But Hergé is still working through the question of his own wartime behaviour, make no mistake. The story begins just as another, the Western film Tintin and Haddock have been watching, ends. As they discuss it leaving the cinema Haddock dismisses it as unrealistic – saying, effectively, that its heroic conventions do not work in the real world. Things are never that neat and tidy, and events are no more likely to unfold 'to order' than, say, General Alcazar, whom he and Tintin have not seen in years, is to pop up on the street corner. Bang on cue, General Alcazar pops up on the street corner. Soon, Tintin and Haddock find themselves in the middle of a situation that the Captain again (and like Hergé himself) dismisses as only happening in works of fiction: enforced mass-transport – not of Jews but of black Africans, pilgrims to Mecca who are destined to be sold as slaves.

As the critic Jean-Marie Apostolidès points out in his 1984 work *Les Metamorphoses de Tintin* (*Tintin's Metamorphoses*), Hergé uses the Red Sea in several overlapping ways. Firstly, to express isolation: Tintin and Haddock float on a raft surrounded by all types of sharks of which the human variety are the worst. Secondly, to reproach the public who read his cartoons during the occupation then denounced him as soon as the liberation came: 'I let you out of that dungeon, and what thanks do I get? You knock me flat!' Haddock shouts at the Africans who mistake him for one of their actual oppressors. He also uses it to realign his world politically: in Skut, the pilot who, as an Estonian, would have fought for the Germans, who initially attacks Tintin and the Captain but ends up befriending them, he brings a former Nazi-accomplice over to the good side. Conversely, by surrounding Rastapopoulos with Nazi colleagues he erodes his Semitic status: he cannot (surely) be Jewish if he mixes with these people, and it follows that Hergé cannot be anti-Semitic in having him as a villain. Tintin and Haddock he allies with the Americans: by staying in radio contact with the U.S.S. *Los Angeles* until its crew turn up and save the day, the duo are playing the role of the *Résistance* – whose coded messages exchanged by wireless with the Allies, incidentally, formed the basis for the radio messages in Cocteau's *Orphée*.

Yet despite these clever rejiggings, Hergé's sense of guilt keeps pulsing through. Castafiore welcomes Tintin and Haddock to the yacht on which Rastapopoulos (or 'di Gorgonzola' as he calls himself) is holding a non-stop fancy-dress ball while simultaneously directing his slave operations (the yacht whose name, *Scheherazade*, is apt given all the fantastic stories and self-perpetuating lies being acted out on it) in the name of 'Art': naïve, compromised art in bed with evil. Castafiore will again play this role in *Tintin and Alph-Art*, inviting Tintin and the Captain to an exclusive party where she confronts them with her new friends Trickler, the devious oil-man from *The Broken Ear*, and Dawson, corrupt chief of police in *The Blue Lotus* and arms trader in *The Red Sea Sharks*. That these unwholesome constellations from the past follow Tintin through the books, refusing to let go, is doubly significant – or, rather, signifies a kind of double-move on Hergé's part: on the one hand, to let the past loom up and accuse him and, on the other, to renounce and discredit the accusers. This is what is going on in the trial sequence of *Tintin and the Picaros*: Hergé allows the trial that never took place in his life to play itself out in his work while at the same time portraying it as a farce, before wiping the whole thing out with a transmission breakdown.

By the 1970s Hergé had reinvented himself as a liberal leftist. He tells Sadoul: 'Economics rule the world; industrial and financial powers condition our way of life. These men obviously don't wear cagoules when they meet in their headquarters, but the result is the same as if they did wear them! Produce, is their first objective. Always produce more. Produce, even if to do this they have to pollute the rivers, the sea, the sky; even if they have to destroy the plants, the forests, the animals. Produce and condition us to make us "consume" more and more, more and more cars, deodorants, spectacles, sex, tourism . . .' 'Is Tintin also against consumer society?' Sadoul asks him. 'Absolutely against it, of course!' Hergé replies. 'Tintin has always taken the side of the oppressed.' There is no reason to doubt that this new-found position is sincere, although it must be admitted that in the media-arts environment of the seventies it was the most convenient place to be, politically speaking, just as collaboration was the most convenient path through the war. Either way, there remains the interesting paradox that, despite his political realignment, Hergé keeps the same villains in place: men in cagoules, the secret cabals of *Cigars of the Pharaoh*, serve as straw men for his leftist world-vision just as well as they did for his rightist one. Through the erasures and rewritings, the same patterns repeat.

ii

Hergé never denied his right-to-left trajectory, but while talking about it he would 'correct' it, presenting it instead as a move away from politics altogether towards an ideology of friendship. The avatar of this ideology, both within and beyond the *Tintin* books, is a Chinese man named Tchang.

As *Cigars of the Pharaoh* drew to a close in the *Petit Vingtième* in 1933, Hergé announced that Tintin's next adventure would take place in the Far East. Shortly thereafter he received a letter from one Abbé Gosset, who looked after Chinese students at the Catholic University of Louvain. 'If you are ill-advised enough to draw a Chinese person with a pigtail,' wrote the Abbé, 'or have him eat birds' nests while emitting little cries of *"Hi! Hi! Hi!"*, you will cause great hurt among my students. Because they read the *Vingtième Siècle* and adore the *Petit Vingtième!*' To prevent stereotypes like these finding their way into the new story, as they had already into *Tintin in the Land of the Soviets* in the form of two pony-tailed Chinese torturers, Gosset proposed to 'lend' Hergé one of his students as an 'advisor'. Hergé accepted the offer, and in May 1934, aged twenty-seven, encountered for the first of many times Tchang Tchong Jen, one year his junior.

Formally, Tchang's impact on Hergé's work was massive. Also an artist, Tchang gave him lessons in Chinese calligraphy, which refined and deepened Hergé's graphic range. He meticulously described the colours and backgrounds of his native Shanghai, down to the signs and slogans that would hang over the streets. This not only helped make *The Blue Lotus* the most visually rich of all the *Tintin* books, but also instilled in Hergé a lasting adherence to verisimilitude: from now on, settings and costumes would have to be *right*. Tchang's impact on Hergé's thinking was also huge. He broke apart Hergé's European absolutism, opening it up into a more global, relative vision: if Europeans see Chinese as cruel baby-killers who bind women's feet, and Chinese are brought up to believe that 'all white devils are wicked', this, as Tintin says in *The Blue Lotus*, carrying Hergé and Tchang's conversations on into the book itself, is because 'different peoples don't know enough about each other'. Over the course of several months during which they met each Sunday, the two men became close, and when the story itself got under way Hergé paid Tchang the ultimate tribute of turning him into one of its main characters, his hero's first true friend.

Tintin may start life as a political agent, but after his meeting with Tchang both he and the work in general increasingly disavow politics in favour of friendship. In the next book, *The Broken Ear*, the underworld henchman Pablo comes to Tintin's rescue when the hero is imprisoned as an enemy of Alcazar's government not because of any political allegiance Pablo holds, but rather for emotional reasons, because he owes Tintin a debt of gratitude for sparing his life earlier. The next time Tintin meets Alcazar, back-stage in the music hall in *The Seven Crystal Balls*, the General has replaced the political hostility he bore Tintin back in San Theodoros with a credo of pure friendship, which he announces in Spanish as he greets Captain Haddock: 'Los amigos de nuestros amigos son nuestros amigos' – 'The friends of our friends are our friends.' In The Calculus Affair Tintin and Haddock travel to Borduria to rescue their friend Calculus, not to fight or expose totalitarianism. In Tintin and the Picaros (Hergé's final complete work) they travel to Los Dopicos and even help the revolution not because they share Alcazar's political vision (whatever that may be) but simply to rescue their friends Thompson and Thomson. Politics is present, but it is treated with disdain. Compare the serious maliciousness with which Stalinism is imbued in Tintin in the Land of the Soviets with the farcical joke it has become in The Calculus Affair, or Tintin's early encounters with the poor of Moscow and Shanghai with his late non-encounter with those of Los Dopicos/Tapiocopolis/Alcazaropolis as he flies over them in the cabin of a jumbo jet in Tintin and the Picaros. What could they have to tell him about the revolution anyway? All it has meant for them is a change of name on the placard beside their hovels and of the uniform worn by the police who swing their truncheons at them.

Politically, Tintin believes in something in Russia and in the Congo; in the sky above the South American shanty towns, no longer. Even as he faces the firing squad on the same coordinates forty years earlier in The Broken Ear, fresh from his meeting with Tchang, he does not believe the slogans he is shouting: he knows and cares nothing about either of San Theodoros's prospective leaders and cries out 'Long live General Alcazar!' by chance, because he is drunk. Friendship may bring about emotional awakening and cultural enlightenment, but politically it brings cynicism.

iii

Hergé 'corrected' himself from right to left, and 'corrected' the left–right opposition itself into a politics–friendship opposition. But if we widen our frame a little, we will see that these are only partial corrections made within the overall structure of a much larger opposition: that between the sacred and the profane.

The extreme right-wing convictions that held sway at the *Vingtième Siècle* were not just political dogmas: they were also sacred beliefs. Royalism was expounded not because it was held to be the most efficient or just system of governance, but rather because the king was a quasi-divine figure, ordained by God himself. Abbé Wallez hated the left because it was anti-God; he hated Jews at a primordial level because they crucified Christ and at a more contemporary one because to his mind Judaism's mercantile values heralded the modern era's replacement of God by capital. When Tintin goes to Russia he goes with a Christian spirit, charitably buying a meal for a beggar (who turns out not to be a beggar after all) while Snowy provides bread for an orphaned child. When he goes to Africa he goes with a missionary spirit, observing the good works that the European priests have carried out, even teaching in their mission school. Indeed, more than just a missionary, he becomes, like Kurtz in Joseph Conrad's 1899 novella *Heart of Darkness*, a kind of god. As Apostolidès points out, this is largely because he 'incarnates the values of the Christian West at a precise moment in history'. He both embodies the modern state (in the newspaper version the Belgian state, in the album version the European one) and enacts what Apostolidès calls its 'need to ground its authority in a transcendence which makes it incontestable' – that is, to link it to the absolute, to God.

This authority may be grounded in the divine, but it is established and consolidated through technology. Tintin manages to divert the arrows the m'Hatouvou tribe fire at him – an act that causes them to fall at his feet in worship – by hiding an electrical magnet behind a tree. He manages to expel the 'evil spirits' inhabiting a sick Babaoro'm hunter, moving the man's wife to prostrate herself before him and proclaim him a 'great sorcerer', by administering quinine. He usurps power from the Babaoro'm tribe's own sorcerer with a gramophone and camera, recording and playing back video and audio footage of the African mocking his followers' ignorance and profaning the fetish they worship. In effect, he plays Prospero to the sorcerer's Sycorax in Shakespeare's *The Tempest*, stealing the native magician's mantle thanks to his superior craft.

At one point in *Tintin au Congo*, the Babaoro'm sorcerer worries aloud that, thanks to Tintin, his people will not listen to him any more. He certainly chooses the right metaphor: throughout the *Tintin* books, sacred authority manifests itself largely as a *voice*, and commanding – or commandeering – that voice is what guarantees power. The tricks Tintin plays in Africa are essentially ones of transmission and reception, and they anticipate the tricks he plays later: when he appears to control the sun simply by speaking to it in *Prisoners of the Sun*, he is actually inserting his voice into the transmission-reception circuit of Inca divinity with the help of modern astronomy (he knows there will be an eclipse at exactly the moment he speaks); when he impersonates God in order to control the mad Philippulus in *The Shooting Star*, casting his voice into the sky around the deranged self-declared prophet, he is doing the same thing to the latter's Christian-psychotic divinity circuit with nothing more than a megaphone.

This strategy may work, but it is dangerous. Why? Because it loosens the lock on the Pandora's box of atheism. Show the 'voice of God' coming through a megaphone, or 'miracles' brought about by machinations, and you have as good as suggested that God could be a con-trick. There is – quite paradoxically given their sacred origins – what we might call a 'profanising' tendency in the *Tintin* books from the outset. In *Tintin in the Land of the Soviets*, as we have already seen, the hero comes across a 'house of spirits' in which ghostly voices warn him not to 'intrude upon the kingdom of the dead'. Terrified at first, he eventually digs up the floorboards and finds a record player. 'Very modern ghosts! They put their voices on gramophone records,' he scoffs to Snowy. The holy world of spirits collapses once we see the mechanisms at work behind it.

As the books develop, the divine gets debunked in other ways as well: through science, commerce, even tourism. When *The Broken Ear*'s sacred fetish goes to Europe it turns into a commodity. When Europe comes to the jungle in the form of the anthropologist Ridgewell it replaces the Arumbayas' sacred ritual with golf and undermines the Rumbabas' tribal rites with a cheap music-hall turn (the ventriloquist's trick through which Ridgewell makes the tribe's totem instruct them to release him and Tintin). The divine counterflows against this profanising current, punches back: as Michel Serres points out, the fetish remains sacred inasmuch as it gives death to those who take it. In the Peruvian books the profane discourse of archaeology is invaded by the arcane craft of voodoo magic and a music-hall performance overtaken by the Sun God, who inserts *his* voice into the mouth of a performer who is amusing godless crowds by listing the contents of their wallets, who asserts *his* power by sending people into deep lethargic trances, starting a trail that will lead from music hall to temple. But overall these are rearguard actions in a larger losing battle.

The sacred and the political are bound together from the outset, as we saw earlier. Throughout the works, political phenomena are imbued with sacred attributes. King Ottokar, like Christ, must undergo three days of withdrawal before showing himself to his people in *King Ottokar's Sceptre*. Tintin, also Christ-like, is paraded (also for three days) through the streets of Shanghai prior to his execution in *The Blue Lotus*. Condemned to the same fate in *The Broken Ear*, he finds himself caught up in a stylised ritual which, mirroring that of the Rumbaba, has sacred overtones: the revolution, like the rites which accompany primitive social processes, calls for sacrifice. It demands blood.

And from the outset, the same tendency towards debasing or debunking plagues the political. The other great incidence of scepticism in *Tintin in the Land of the Soviets* is a good example of this. Tintin comes across a group of English communists being shown a factory in the healthy throes of full production; deciding to investigate from closer up, he discovers that its buildings are no more than stage fronts, its smoke made by burning straw, the din of its 'machines' by a man hammering a strip of sheet metal. 'That's how the Soviets fool the poor idiots who still believe in a "Red Paradise",' says Tintin, using a holy language of belief and heaven while simultaneously 'emptying' it out: the 'paradise' is fake, the belief misguided. In *Tintin in America* social and political processes are also revealed as mere charades: 'justice' requires the lynching of innocents; bank managers steal money; the enforcers of the Prohibition law get drunk. The sacred is *itself* presented as a swindle: 'Profit from our new religion! Join the Brothers of Neo-judeo-buddho-islamo-americanism, and earn the highest dividends in the world!' a proselytiser tells Tintin, waving a recruitment leaflet. The book's 'Grynde' sequence, in which Tintin visits the aptly named meat-plant, is taken straight from Georges Duhamel's 1930 book *America the*

Menace: Scenes from the Life of the Future. In a chapter entitled 'The Kingdom of Death' Duhamel describes slaughter not as a sacred sacrificial ritual but as a profane, degraded process: blood falls from the animals not as a libation for the gods but rather 'to be made into I don't know what – food, drugs, jewels, explosives'. The very notion of transcendence is slaughtered along with the cows, and the smell of this slaughter 'flows back toward the heart of the city, and, tenaciously mingled with the atmosphere, with human beings, and with thoughts, seems the natural and intimate odour of American luxury'.

Guy Debord, the figurehead of the radical artistic and political movement Situationism, claimed in the sixties that power establishes and asserts itself through spectacle. Shakespeare knew this long before him: towards the end of *The Tempest* the power that Prospero has usurped from Sycorax is cemented through a spectacular masque, a breathtaking performance full of spirits and illusions which captivates and holds in awe all the island's inhabitants. The masque, and hence the power that it consolidates, is vulnerable to two threats. The first, more obvious one comes from Prospero's political rivals: he neutralises this threat by having his spirit agents stupefy and confuse them. The second one, which takes him by surprise, comes from the bumbling clowns Trinculo, Stephano and Caliban, who disrupt (if only momentarily) his whole master-plan when they interrupt his masque, stumbling drunkenly onto the stage.

The *Tintin* books are full of spectacles which both strengthen political power and put it at risk: the King having to parade his sceptre through the streets of Klow, risking forced abdication if he cannot hold it up for all the crowds to see; the Maharaja riding elephant-back through avenues thronged with his subjects, vulnerable to his enemies' poisoned arrows; the Inca ceremony in which the all-powerful Inca ends up pleading for clemency from his intended victim. Virtually every one of Hergé's spectacles is, like Prospero's masque, interrupted in some way or other. Sometimes the interruptions are innocuous; sometimes they are not. On occasion the deadly serious can hide in the innocuous: General Tapioca thinks in *Tintin and the Picaros* that his agents have stupefied his opponents with a thousand air-dropped crates of whisky, but they come in (at his own invitation) in clown outfits, and unseat him.

In the *Tintin* books you find 'full' spectacles containing genuine, rich layers of social meaning – the Inca ritual, the sceptre-trooping – and 'empty' spectacles that are no more than hollow shams: Soviet production; the attack on a fake, model city in *The Calculus Affair*; the simulated attack on the base of the pyramid in *Tintin and the Picaros*; the contrived charade of the trial in the same book. Full and empty spectacle make move and counter-move against one another, but the empty wins out in the long run. By *The Castafiore Emerald* the media is itself an empty spectacle: everything within it is either false, as with the magazine feature whose claims are entirely groundless, or, as with the television recording sequence, constructed, staged, played out to order under artificial lights (which does not stop it being interrupted: in releasing the parrot into the room

Haddock plays the role of Situationist prankster). *Tintin and the Picaros* perfectly illustrates, as Michel Serres points out, Debord's notion of the 'Society of the Spectacle': its hotel room is a mediated stage set, surveilled and controlled from all angles. But where Debord's statements and analyses formed part of a committed revolutionary programme, Hergé's Situationism hollows out Situationism itself, reducing ideology, as a reviewer pointed out when the book appeared in 1976, to décor, hollow as Soviet factory fronts.

Fine, a humanist might say: as we learnt earlier, Hergé doesn't believe in politics any more because now he believes in friendship. Yet it seems that we might have to correct this too. The dreadful truth is that, over the course of the books, friendship gradually becomes as hollowed-out as politics. It, too, follows the sacred-to-profane trajectory. Tintin's friendship with Tchang is utterly sacred. It even has its own spirit-frequency of transmission – one picked up by only Tintin and the blind monk Blessed Lightning in their visions. Hergé describes *Tintin in Tibet* to Sadoul as 'a hymn to friendship'. At its conclusion, Tintin receives a formal blessing from a holy order for the strength and tenacity of his friendship, a blessing that takes the form of a spectacle which (of course) is interrupted, by the Captain blowing into the ceremonial trumpet.

But, for Hergé, friendship has had a worm in its core since as early as *The Broken Ear*, whose fetish is a gauge of friendship between the Walker expedition and the Arumbaya tribe – a friendship that turns very sour. Fast-forward to *The Red Sea Sharks*, and Skut's loyalty to his new friends Tintin and the Captain. When the ship on which they are held captive catches fire the villains try to persuade Skut to leave with them, but he refuses because, as he explains to Tintin and the Captain, 'I want to . . . er . . . wake you . . . and send radio signal . . .' Why the hesitation? Was his priority really to save them, or was he more concerned with the radio? By *Flight 714* the Captain's friendship with Professor Calculus is flagging. By *Tintin and the Picaros* there is constant arguing and bickering: between Haddock and Calculus, Haddock and Tintin, Calculus and the other two. Alcazar reuses his *amigos* line in this book – but this time he uses it insincerely, strategically, cranking it out for Jolyon Wagg as he plans to steal his coach and Jolly Folly outfits so he can drive to Los Dopicos and seize power again: friendship has become an empty ideology, the currency with which to buy something else. Most telling of all, Pablo reappears, ostensibly to save Tintin once more by warning him of an imminent assassination attempt, but in reality to lure him into one, using his debt of friendship itself as the false badge of his sincerity: dirty money.

From sacred fascism to sacred friendship to hollow, profane versions of both: this is the path traced by Hergé through the refracted twentieth century of the *Tintin* books. Towards the end of his life, depressed again, he felt a growing longing for his old friend Tchang, whom he had not seen since the 1930s. He spent years trying to track him down, to no avail. Eventually, in the late seventies, he received word of him. Tchang had returned to Shanghai, founded an art school on the European model, been sent to a 're-education' camp during the Cultural Revolution, survived and returned to Shanghai, where he was still living. A few years later, after intense rounds of diplomatic and commercial negotiations, the two men were reunited. The reunion took place in March 1981, at Zaventem Airport. Hergé was extremely famous by this point, and the event unfolded in front of a huge crowd of journalists, who captured his anticipation as Tchang's plane taxied across the runway and then filmed the two men embracing, as arranged, beneath a large *Tintin in Tibet* poster, exchanging the words spoken between Tchang and Tintin on their reunion in the book: 'I knew I'd find you in the end! . . . This is wonderful!' 'Tintin! Oh, how often I've thought of you!' They were then whisked off for a round of television appearances in which musicians got up as the Marlinspike Prize Band played waltzes as they marched around studios designed in collaboration with Hergé's publisher Casterman's marketing men.

Hergé looked ill throughout. He had leukaemia: his blood was failing him, making him anaemic. Tchang looked confused. Eventually, after a few more rounds of stage-managed spectacles, he was whisked back home to totalitarian China. 'They're pining for you in Borduria,' Tintin tells Sponsz as he removes his Jolly Folly mask after the coup at the end of *Tintin and the Picaros*. Sponsz, too, has a plane waiting for him. He will not face the firing squad because Tintin has extracted from Alcazar a guarantee that there will be no executions in this revolution. Its blood, too, will fail it: it will be anaemic. 'But General,' Colonel Alvarez exclaims when he hears this, 'it's contrary to every custom . . . The people will be terribly disappointed . . .' Even Tapioca pleads: 'For pity's sake, don't pardon me! Do you want me completely dishonoured?' But Alcazar apologetically explains that he is bound, adding with a sigh: 'We live in sad times!' Too right.

3

PLACE OF DEAD MEN, HERE: FROM CHÂTEAU TO CRYPT AND BACK AGAIN

Haddock Goes to Heaven, Simon English, 2005.

i

Tintin is always entering tombs. Egyptian pyramids, Inca *chulpas*, hidden burial chambers: he seems drawn to these places like a dowser's stick to subterranean water. He floats in a sarcophagus and lies in a grave, presumed dead both times. Even spaces not designed for burial turn into tombs when he steps into them: a secret cavern under the American prairie is transformed into a sepulchre for him as the Blackfoot Indians haul a boulder over its entrance and declare: 'No way out but death.' A whole bunker-filled South Pacific atoll is taken over and ear-marked as his vault by Rastapopoulos, who tells him: 'this island will be your grave!'

The tombs that Tintin penetrates are usually exotic ones in far-flung places. But perhaps the most important one of all is located no more than a few kilometres from his home in Labrador Road. After a scene halfway through *The Secret of the Unicorn* which reprises many of the elements of the first burial sequence in *Cigars of the Pharaoh* (he is drugged, packaged and transported in both), Tintin comes round to find himself walled up in the cellar of Marlinspike Hall. His temporary vault this time turns out to form part not just of the catacomb of an old church, but also of the ancestral ground of Captain Haddock. Like Balzac's *Sarrasine*, in which the provenance of the Adonis painting is tied in with the history of the de Lanty family in whose house it hangs (la Zambinella, it transpires, is their still-living relative), Hergé's plot opens up into a complex family story.

Tintin's own family is conspicuously absent throughout the whole *oeuvre*. So is that of Calculus, who vehemently protests that he does not have and never had a sister when he mishears 'missed a . . .' and 'insist . . . er . . .' in *Tintin and the Picaros*. Haddock, by contrast, is introduced in *The Crab with the Golden Claws* crying for his mother. Two adventures later his family provides the plot of the diptych *The Secret of the Unicorn–Red Rackham's Treasure*, in the first section of which the cellar scene takes place. Let's backtrack from this scene to an earlier passage of the book: spurred into curiosity by Tintin's gift to him of a model of the boat his ancestor Sir Francis Haddock commanded back in the seventeenth century, the Captain digs out his ancestor's memoirs and reads them over the course of a night and the next day, drinking furiously as he does so. They reveal that Sir Francis's ship, the *Unicorn*, was taken over by the pirate Red Rackham after a battle during which the pirate's ship was sunk. Red Rackham slaughtered the *Unicorn*'s crew, took Sir Francis prisoner and transferred the treasure he had previously plundered from another ship onto the *Unicorn*. But Sir Francis escaped and blew his own ship up with the gunpowder in its hold, killing all the pirates while he himself found refuge on a nearby island. Returning to Europe years later, Sir Francis made three models of the *Unicorn*, and bequeathed one to each of his three sons, instructing them all, in writing, to adjust its mast.

Why? Because the masts contain parchments, each of which bears a text declaring that three unicorns 'sailing in the noonday Sunne' – *le Soleil de midi* – 'will speak. For 'tis from the Light that Light will dawn.' When the parchments are overlaid and held up to a light source, they reveal the co-ordinates of Red Rackham's treasure. Tintin, after escaping from the vault in which we left him, holding the overlaid parchments up to a light bulb and noting down the coordinates, sets out with the Captain for the Caribbean to look for the treasure, picking Calculus and his prototype shark-submarine up en route. They return without finding it, but having instead discovered among the skulls and cannons of the *Unicorn*'s wreck on the seabed scraps of paper which, when pieced together by Calculus, reconstitute a deed with which King Louis XIV (for reasons that will soon become bright as the noonday sun, the English translators' substitution of Charles II is woefully inadequate) legated to 'our trusty and beloved knight, Francis Haddock' – *notre cher et aimé François, Chevalier de Hadoque* – the very same Marlinspike Hall in whose cellar Tintin found himself walled up. As its former owners, the Bird Brothers, have been sent to prison thanks to Tintin, the Hall is now up for sale. Since Calculus has sold the patent for his submarine and has money, he buys the Hall back for the Captain. It is there, in the catacomb itself, that they find the treasure, hidden inside a globe which opens when the spot indicated by the parchments' coordinates is pressed. The Captain, who has both found his ancestor's treasure and reclaimed his family estate – *château de mes ancêtres* – announces at the book's end, as he opens in Marlinspike's newly named Maritime Gallery a permanent exhibition of the journals, model *Unicorns* and real *Unicorn*'s mast and anchor: 'All's well that ends well' – a statement so final that he has to repeat it two more times.

Calculus, Tintin and Haddock spend hours scrutinising the story's various scraps of paper. But the psychoanalyst Serge Tisseron, whom we met earlier, has looked even closer and found another secret hidden in them. In the seventeenth century it was conventional for the monarch to give property to his illegitimate offspring in lieu of recognition. Tisseron's suspicion that this convention might lie behind Louis XIV's gift to his 'beloved' Francis is confirmed when he notices, near the beginning of the book that immediately follows *Red Rackham's Treasure*, *The Seven Crystal Balls*, a dolphin-and-crown blazon carved above the château's front door: the sign of the dauphin, heir to the throne. The symbol is explicit and unambiguous, and too glaring to have found its way onto Marlinspike's façade by accident: it can only signal royal filiation. Its presence must mean either that the château was initially intended for Louis's official heir (and given tacitly to his unofficial one) or that Sir Francis, denied his birthright, has carved it in mute protest. Either way, as Tisseron points out in a second book he wrote on this subject, his 1993 *Tintin et le Secret d'Hergé* (*Tintin and the Secret of Hergé*), 'the "treasure" hidden in the foundations of his "house" is nothing other than the secret of an exceptional ascendance' – that is, the secret that Sir Francis is Louis XIV's unrecognised son.

While it is possible that Sir Francis is not himself aware of this, Tisseron suspects that he is very much aware of it and has used the material treasure to put his children onto the trail of the immaterial secret. Louis XIV was known as *le Roi Soleil* or 'Sun King': in Sir Francis's diction of noonday sun – *Soleil de midi* – and light issuing forth from light, Louis's paternal, generative presence is all but spelt out. Yet Tintin, who (when interpreting degrees of longitude) has corrected London to Paris and (when interpreting what these corrected coordinates *really* mean) has corrected world to map, still misses the real secret of the *Unicorn*, dazzled by the treasure into falling for the same trick the Egyptians loved to play on the Egyptologists they knew would one day come and penetrate their tombs: the dummy- or double-chamber.

ii

But there is still one more chamber hidden among Marlinspike's foundations – or, rather, a parallel secret tomb or cavern buried in the real world. Hergé's grandmother, Marie Dewigne, was a maid in a château not unlike Marlinspike: that of the Comtesse Errembault de Dudzeele, at Chaumont-Gistoux, a village thirty kilometres from

Brussels. In 1882 she gave birth out of wedlock, to a father who did not come forward and stand by her, to twin boys, Léon and Alexis, Hergé's uncle and father respectively. The next year the Comtesse pushed Marie into a 'white marriage' with the château's gardener, Philippe Remi, who would stand in as the children's official 'father'. The 'couple' did not even live together, and when Philippe left the Comtesse's employ a short while later, Marie found herself abandoned for a second time. Nonetheless, Alexis and Léon were well taken care of by the Comtesse, who made sure they always had fine clothes and were well educated, just like young aristocrats. As soon as they reached the age of fourteen, though, she did a sudden U-turn, and the boys were turfed out of the château to eke out a petit-bourgeois existence in the world beyond its gates.

Hergé never discussed this beyond his family circle. It was not until after his death in 1983 that the information reached the public domain. When it did, his biographers asked the obvious question: who was Alexis and Léon's real father? But to no avail. All they could ascertain was that it was 'someone who used to pass by the château'. It could have been a trades-man. It could equally have been an aristocrat. The King himself was one of the Comtesse's regular visitors. The father's real identity will almost certainly never be known – but what the biographers did find out was that the 'Remi' family (they kept the gardener's name if nothing else) liked to believe the aristocratic, and perhaps even the royal, version. According to Hervé Springaël's 1987 biography, Hergé once told his cousin: 'I won't tell you who our grandfather is, because it would go to your head.' Thierry Smolderen and Pierre

Sterckx, writing one year later, attribute this line to Alexis and Léon, who told their own children (and here the minute variation is worthy of Thompson and Thomson): 'We won't tell you who your grandfather was; it would turn your head.'

Once we know this family story, how can we keep it off the radar when we think of the tacit complicity with royalty Tintin shows throughout the books? How can we not hear some echo of it each time Tintin goes and deposits another abandoned child in a home? He installs the orphaned Tchang in Wang-Chen-yee's house in *The Blue Lotus*, sees the street-urchin Zorrino welcomed into the Inca temple in *Prisoners of the Sun* and returns the gypsy girl Miarka to her family whom the Captain then 'adopts' wholesale in *The Castafiore Emerald*. When Abdullah, a royal child, turns up in Marlinspike unwanted in *The Red Sea Sharks*, the Captain finds himself in the Comtesse's shoes, and keeps him grudgingly for as long as he has to. Thompson and Thomson, twins (or are they? do their very names not suggest that they have two 'fathers'?), are (as Tisseron also notices) mocked time and again for wearing the wrong clothes – or rather for wearing the 'right' ones (Chinese national costumes in China or Swiss ones in Switzerland). When asked by Sadoul where the inspiration for them came from Hergé talks immediately of Alexis and Léon, describing their moustaches and bowler hats. He then – bizarrely – claims that he was not thinking of them when he created the detectives. But how is it possible not to pick up in the coupling of their pompous diction and their constant malapropisms an anxiety about levels of education, snobbery mixed with insecurity? How can we not see a shadow of the real twins' expulsion in the books, played out not just once but again and again? American Indians are expelled from their ancestral ground, Alcazar and the Emir from their palaces; Haddock is usurped and cast adrift from his own boat, just as Sir Francis was. The same gang who do this to him in *The Crab with the Golden Claws* later offload him, in *The Red Sea Sharks*, from the glamorous *Scheherazade* to the grubby *Ramona*: like Alexis and Léon, he finds himself trading down homes against his will.

'Someone who used to pass by the château': if there is one set-up that is absolutely instrumental in driving Hergé's plots, it is the relationship between host and guest. At best this relationship is fraught; at worst it goes disastrously wrong. In *The Broken Ear*'s back-story story the Arumbaya tribe treat Walker's expedition 'very well' and let them stay, but when it transpires that the expedition's interpreter has stolen a sacred diamond the Arumbayas hunt them down and massacre them. In *King Ottokar's Sceptre* Alembick, the visiting sigillographer, is afforded every courtesy by his Syldavian hosts, and even allowed into their inner Treasure Chamber – until he steals the royal sceptre and is imprisoned. In *Tintin and the Picaros* the relationship between the San Theodorian regime and their guests Tintin, Haddock and Calculus breaks down completely, so much so that the visitors' 'cold cynicism' is denounced to the whole nation on television. This breakdown is a classical one: ever since Oedipus's father Laius betrayed the bond of hospitality by raping his host Pelops's son it has provided authors with dynamic situations. Look at Shakespeare's *Macbeth* – and in particular the lines Macduff screams when he finds King Duncan murdered by his host ('O horror, horror, horror!'); then flip to the sequence in *Tintin au Congo* in which the Babaoro'm sorcerer 'finds' the tribe's sacred fetish with its head staved in and cries out 'Horror and sacrilege!' Look at the arguments which follow King Lear's arrival as a guest at Regan's castle with his over-staffed retinue (Do you need so many servants? she keeps asking him. Do you even need one?); then open *The Castafiore Emerald* to the page where the diva, arriving unin-vited with her entourage at Marlinspike, explains that 'we didn't have to ring' – to which Haddock replies: '"We"? There can't be more than one of you!' There is.

Troubled host–guest relationships crop up again and again in *Tintin*, on small levels as well as grand ones. Tintin mis-takes the hospitality of Pygmies for aggression in Africa and the aggression of Red Indians for hospitality in America. He, Haddock and Calculus are unwilling guests of Laszlo Carreidas in his supersonic jet in *Flight 714* and unwilling hosts, repeatedly, of the vulgar and uncultivated Jolyon Wagg, who keeps barging into Marlinspike, even installing his whole family there at one point. Waking up in Wang-Chen-yee's house after being chloroformed and kidnapped in *The Blue Lotus*, Tintin thinks he is a prisoner but turns out to be an honoured guest (albeit one whose host's first gesture is to express shame at the manner of his summoning). In the Szohôd Hotel of *The Calculus Affair* it is the other way round: he and the Captain are *treated* as honoured guests but are in fact prisoners of the police state ('Let's talk about the simply wonderful hospitality of this exquisite country,' Tintin says to

Haddock on the room-to-room telephone, fully aware the line is tapped). The host–guest relationship is fraught in the same book in the Bordurian embassy in Rolle, where diplomatic status provides cover for the spiriting away of a scientist, Calculus, whom Borduria will later claim to have 'invited' to their country, just as it is fraught in *The Blue Lotus* in the international concession in Shanghai, whose chief of police has constantly to negotiate terms with the occupying army that surrounds him – embassies and concessions being official footholds of the guest in a host nation. It is even fraught in the Syldavian restaurant in (not quite) Brussels in *King Ottokar's Sceptre*, where Tintin, the guest of guests, is handed a 'proverb' telling him to keep his nose out of others' affairs. 'We shan't see him again in a hurry!' the waiter laughs after shocking him by telling him he has just been served dog – before discovering that Snowy has ransacked his kitchen. A few days later Tintin reads a travel brochure emphasising Syldavian hospitality; the Bordurians seem to have read it too, taken it the wrong way and prepared to move in. 'Invitation? You mean invasion!' scoffs the Captain when asked by journalists in *Tintin and the Picaros* about Castafiore's visit to Marlinspike in the preceding adventure, *The Castafiore Emerald*. The only people he actually invited were the gypsies, those perennial unwanted guests, and they passed on before taking their leave – only to be caught up with and held against their will.

'Someone who used to pass by the château.' A noble, perhaps even royal guest of the Comtesse Errembault de Dudzeele fathered Alexis and Léon but refused to recognise them: that is the story the Remi family hoarded like a buried treasure to be both ashamed and proud of. And that is the story Hergé has made a parallel version of and buried it among the parchments, treasure and château of *The Secret of the Unicorn*. It is the story Sir Francis has written between the lines of his own texts but has not managed to make legible: he may be illegitimate but his descendants are, like Bab El Ehr's men, illiterate. In *Red Rackham's Treasure* this story is dug up and buried in one and the same movement: Louis XIV, the *Roi Soleil* or Sun King, disappears at the very moment he becomes visible, hiding in the midday sun itself.

The story that follows, the double-book adventure *The Seven Crystal Balls* and *Prisoners of the Sun*, may seem to strike off on a completely different route, but this is simply sleight of hand. Tintin arrives at the *château de mes ancêtres* in which the Captain has now installed himself after their trip to the watery burial ground of the *Unicorn*, and waits beneath the dauphin-blazon (which even has twin boys carved in the stone above it) before being admitted. On his train journey there he reads about another penetration of a tomb, that of the Incas, and has an over-the-shoulder reader comment that this is shoddy behaviour on the part of the archaeologist guests. The Peruvian hosts think so too, and have come as guests to Europe ('passing by' with a music-hall show) to wreak vengeance. Calculus, who starts the book looking for an Ur-European tomb, is punished for unwittingly donning royal clothes by being kidnapped and taken to the temple that the Incas have decided will be his tomb. Tintin and Haddock follow, entering the temple through a burial chamber ('place of dead men' as Zorrino calls it) which, again, is covered by water. They are held as prisoners but treated as honoured guests. In whose name? Whose legacy demands this? The Sun God, the 'sovereign star' – or, to give it another name, the *Roi Soleil*, which ends up eclipsing itself at the vital moment. It is the same story all over again. The tomb was Ur-European after all. And the secret, once more, has been disguised in a name and transplanted across the world to throw its pursuers off the fact that it was right at home the whole time. It is in the home, it is under it, it *is* the home.

For the philosopher Gaston Bachelard, mankind's thoughts, memories and dreams are integrated by a single structure: the house. In his wonderful 1957 book *The Poetics of Space* he several times cites Sigmund Freud's notion, drawn from the stories of E. T. A. Hoffmann, of the Uncanny, pointing out that uncanny things are in fact precisely those that are most 'homely', strangely familiar. Tintin, like Bachelard, studies architecture. When he and the Captain arrive at Professor Topolino's house in *The Calculus Affair* he goes and inspects the back while Haddock rings the doorbell. 'Come back! There's someone here!' calls Haddock, who is surprised when the door opens to find Tintin himself behind it. The two of them then creep around like Egyptologists, disconcerted by familiar things: the radio, the vacuum cleaner, brooms and buckets. Descending into the cellar, they find the house's rightful owner downgraded to below deck as it were, tied up, a prisoner in his own home. The pre-Colombian expert Tarragon is also a prisoner in his home in *The Seven Crystal Balls*: the last member of the Peruvian expedition who has not yet been thrown into a trance, he lives surrounded by armed police, unable to venture out. Tintin inspects his house as well, inquiring about the doors and windows. He, Haddock and Calculus all sleep there and all have a dream straight out of Hoffmann in which an Inca mummy creeps in through the window. Waking from it, they tiptoe around the landing, also disturbed by domestic features such as carpets and potted plants. But the trance-inducing visitor has already passed, via the chimney, and although delayed by a well-aimed shot, he escapes – through the garden's gazebo, a mini-house on the border of the estate that opens both ways, in and out – leaving Tarragon a psychic prisoner, and Calculus a physical one.

'Home sweet home,' sneers Alan as he locks them in an old Japanese bunker in *Flight 714*. In *The Castafiore Emerald* the Captain's home becomes a bunker to which he is confined to sit out wave after wave of assaults by unwanted visitors ('How did you get in?' he asks Castafiore twice on her arrival, ignoring all civilities). The whole book takes place within a radius of no more than a kilometre from his armchair. To write it, Hergé had to make a model of the house. He plays it like an instrument, hitting the keys in modulating sequences as he moves from the staircase to the windows to the attic to the staircase again. In contrast to the treasure-books, the cellar is not shown in this one: this is because the secret buried in it has moved up into the main house and been put on display in the Maritime Gallery while still remaining hidden. The whole house has become a big burial chamber. Professor Calculus's complaint (again, inadequately rendered in the English) that 'Everything is hidden from me in this house!'

needs to be listened to more carefully: 'Everything is hidden from me *in this house*' – it is in this house that everything is hidden from me. Haddock, like Tarragon and his fellow expedition-members, lies in its master bedroom tossing, prey to dreadful dreams.

iii

It is a sign of Hergé's brilliance that he can so seamlessly overlay the architectural, familial, historical, linguistic and psychological strata of his work. This almost instinctive skill is very much appreciated by two more psychoanalysts, Nicholas Abraham and Maria Torok – not in Hergé but in the confused mind of a Russian neurotic named Sergei Pankajev. Tisseron mentions Abraham and Torok's work only in passing, leaving the bulk of it uncovered. But if we stop and disinter it properly, we will find that it throws a huge amount of light across the *Tintin* books.

Published in 1976, Abraham and Torok's book *The Wolf Man's Magic Word: A Cryptonomy* contains – like *Sarrasine*, like *The Secret of the Unicorn* – an embedded family story. It also involves, like Thompson and Thomson's actions in the desert, a reading of a reading. The original reading is Freud's, and the original story is of the patient he nicknamed 'The Wolf Man'. Sergei Pankajev grew up wealthy in a château on a big family estate, surrounded by servants, a nursemaid and a gardener (he would later lose all that and end up working as a clerk). As a toddler, he developed an overwhelming fear of wolves after his sister showed him a picture of one reared up in their playroom. He also experienced a sudden fear of a yellow-striped butterfly he was once chasing, and started habitually mutilating insects. His sister, a gifted naturalist who could list the names of butterflies and who also composed poems which their father compared to those of Lermontov, seduced him as a child, playing with his penis while telling him lewd stories about the maid and the gardener. She later poisoned herself; later still the father did the same. Sergei felt no sorrow at her death but found himself overcome by grief for that of Lermontov when he visited the poet's grave near the River Tierek a year on. Years of intermittent breakdowns followed, accompanied by a compulsive predilection for copulating with women from behind and having enemas administered to himself. Nor was his mental health improved by the death of his wife Teresa (who had been his nurse in one of his asylums), also through self-poisoning.

Freud presents himself in his own study of Pankajev, which he published in 1914 under the title *Notes on a Case of Obsessional Neurosis (The Wolf Man)*, as a psychic archaeologist. He talks of childhood as a 'prehistoric period' and compares Pankajev's mental life to the culture of ancient Egypt, which 'preserves the earlier stages of its development side by side with the end-products, retains the most ancient gods and their attributes along with the most modern ones,

and thus, as it were, spreads out upon a two dimensional surface what other instances of evolution show us in the solid'.
The surfaces of Sergei's mind are like the walls of a pyramid –
the inside walls, covered in hieroglyphics that are both visible
and inscrutable at the same time. In the course of his analysis
Freud studies these, following lines of association from the
reared-up wolf in the sister's drawing to the sexual position of
his father when Sergei once watched him copulating (from
behind) with his mother, to fairy tales read to Sergei in which
wolves lost their tails, to a dream of six white wolves looking at
him from a tree, to an epidemic which killed hundreds of
white sheep that used to roam the family estate; from the
yellow-striped butterfly (in Russian *babushka*, 'granny') to a
store-room in the château full of yellow-striped pears, *grusha*,
to an old maid named Grusha whom Sergei once found
scrubbing the floor, kneeling in the same position as his
mother in the sexual scene; and so on. The real breakthrough
comes when, telling Freud about a dream in which he is torturing a yellow-striped wasp, Sergei mistakenly pronounces
the German word for wasp, *Wespe*, as *Espe*, thus pronouncing
his own initials, SP. This little slip of the tongue acts as a kind
of Rosetta Stone for Freud, allowing him to understand the
whole tangled web of mental associations. Armed with this
codex, he reveals that at the heart of Sergei's neurosis lies a raft
of his own secret desires (for his father, mother and sister) and
fears (of castration and death) that have been bound together
by an elaborate set of connections – connections that are in
turn reactivated and perpetuated through his compulsive
behaviour.

What Freud does, essentially, is decode. Like Tintin, he reads across (from word to object and vice versa) and through (from one episode, one era, to another). Sergei's mind is like the Caribbean Sea in *Red Rackham's Treasure*, with more than one time-zone overlaid in strange simultaneity. His whole life is like the desert in *Land of Black Gold*, a field of almost abject repetition. Freud, like Tintin, understands both these facts. But when Abraham and Torok enter the fray, it gets even more interesting. For them, the trauma in Sergei's past coupled with his failure to mourn his sister has opened up a space within him which is not his own, a chink through which 'the stranger enters the ego, lodged there like a cyst'. Throughout their book they use a barrage of architectural metaphors to describe Sergei's mind: enclaves, partition walls, barriers. At the heart of all this psychic architecture, they decide, is a space of burial – but one whose inhabitant, not having been accorded proper burial rites, is neither properly dead nor properly alive.

Here we are very close to the topography of Tintin's tombs and burials, his 'deaths'. Here, also, with the 'stranger's' penetration of one's 'home' space, we are close to not just the numerous host–guest encounters but also the instances of stowaways that keep cropping up in the books: the clandestine passenger who lurks below the deck of Tintin's ship in *Tintin au Congo*; Calculus hidden away beneath the *Sirius*'s lifeboat's tarpaulin in *Red Rackham's Treasure*; Jorgen skulking in the rocket's hold in *Explorers on the Moon* – not to mention the thief lodged in the museum in *The Broken Ear*; the Italian photographer sneaked into the house in *The Castafiore*

Emerald; and Tintin himself as he clings to the back of Mitsuhirato's car or secretes himself in an oil-drum on the same villain's truck in *The Blue Lotus*. Abraham and Torok's family burial chamber is guarded by psychic 'ghosts'. So is the catacomb at Marlinspike, where Tintin hears the voice of 'the ghost of the captain of the *Unicorn*', or the spot where Sir Francis's idol is found in *Red Rackham's Treasure*, where Thompson and Thomson gibber, 'This island is h-h-haunted, Captain!' after realising that the voice they have just heard is not one of their companions'. Of course, the first 'ghost' is Max Bird's voice piped in through a tube, the second a parrot – but in a non-paranormal way an unquiet spectre really does hang over these grounds on which a family drama of unaccorded rites has been played out.

Abraham and Torok, like Freud (who claims that the failure to mourn produces melancholia, a complex that 'behaves like an open wound', infecting the whole psyche), use a rhetoric of poisonous cysts and infection to describe Pankajev's pathology. If the spectre of madness haunts his life, it hangs over the *Tintin oeuvre* like a pall. Try to count the number of characters who go or are sent mad, or the number of times Tintin is threatened with madness, and you will lose count after the first four or five books. In the two-part story *The Cigars of the Pharaoh–The Blue Lotus* alone, no fewer than four people are struck by arrows dipped in Raijajah, 'the poison of madness'; escorting two of these to an insane asylum in whose gardens patients are shown cavorting and posturing (madness, for Hergé, often leads its victims to believe they are royal personages: Rameses the Second, Napoleon and so on),

Tintin is himself thrown into a strait-jacket and sectioned; later, as Mitsuhirato prepares to inject him with Raijajah, he wails: 'Mad! . . . I'm going to go mad!' Biographically, this is perhaps not unconnected to the fact that Hergé's own mother finished her days in an asylum. In the work itself, though, madness is associated not only with poison, royalty and burial (go too near to the tomb and you risk going mad, like the Egyptologist Sophocles Sarcophagus), but also with stars, balls of fire and the sun. In *The Shooting Star* Tintin sees a vast ball of fire with a spider in it – a traditional symbol of madness; Philippulus the astronomer has spent too much time staring at stars and gone insane, climbing up towards the sun itself ('Higher and higher!' he shouts. 'That is my watchword!'). The Captain thinks Tintin has gone mad when he addresses the sun directly in *Prisoners of the Sun*, then when he sees the darkness move across its face, asks 'Have I gone crazy too?' Of course, as we know, the sun and burial are not so very far apart in Hergé's work; what Tintin enters in Peru is the tomb of the sun itself – that is, metaphorically at least (and we will return to metaphors and the sun later), the unmarked family tomb of Haddock. En route to it he encounters infection, or at least its spectre: the *Pachacamac*, the boat named after the Sun God on which the tomb-hunting Calculus is shipped to South America, is found to carry yellow fever and quarantined 'to avoid risk of infection'. The doctor who makes the diagnosis is, of course, a secret member of the sun cult.

Most interestingly, Abraham and Torok describe pathology in terms of *voice* and *speech*. The Wolf Man's mind, they argue, is conducting a complex conversation with itself, in more than one language; it is not just (as Freud thought) legible but also *audible* – albeit at a pitch beneath the register of actual speech. They describe thousands of ears, their own included, listening to Freud's listening to his patient – another double-eavesdropping – and suggest that the job of the psychoanalyst is not interpreting but translating. Discovering that Pankajev learnt English as well as Russian in his childhood before picking up the German with which he communicates with Freud, they are led to a polyglottal zone of words which they describe as 'crackling'. Behind these crackling words, they say, are buried 'source-words' or 'archaeonyms' which broadcast on illicit mental frequencies. Abraham and Torok tune into these, and are led from 'six', the number of wolves in the dream, to *shiest* ('six' in Russian) and on to *siestra* and *siestorka*, a group of six, and thence, picking up some interference from the German *Schwester*, to the English 'sister' – a world of 'locutions' that 'signal pleasure and allude to the sexual seduction scene'. Words like these they call 'cryptonyms (words that hide)', adding that 'the presence of the cryptonym signals the existence of a crypt'.

A *crypt*: this is the name Abraham and Torok give the non-place at the heart of their thought. It is a loaded term that binds the architecture of burial to the language of secrets. Their crypt encrypts (both 'crypt' and 'encryption' come from the Greek word *kryptos*, 'hidden'). It buries and, in doing so, generates noise, coded speech. The crypt is resonant. It is also porous: its secret words can travel (in, for example, the number of wolves in a dream) through the partitions between the conscious and the unconscious – provided they are encrypted. They can also travel onwards, hidden on the underside of actual speech or via actions which perform them while still leaving them encrypted (such as, for example, torturing an insect), out into the world. The crypt's walls are broken; it oozes; it *transmits*.

Whether or not Abraham and Torok are 'right' about the actual nature of the illness of a man they never met is irrelevant. What is important for us, here, is the model they are proposing. The crypt perfectly names the phenomenon we keep encountering in the *Tintin* books – a crypt that oozes, crackles and transmits to every corner of the work. Let's go back to the family catacomb (or as the Captain calls it in the original French, *crypte*) in Marlinspike. When Tintin breaches its wall with a beam of wood, he immediately hears an eerie sound, old music trickling out (it turns out that he has knocked over an antique music box), just as he hears 'unearthly music' trickling through the wall of the Maharaja's palace to signal the imminent madness-poisoning which is the latter's family legacy in *Cigars of the Pharaoh* (both the Maharaja's father and brother were sent mad). In that book, as we have already seen, Tintin lies in a coffin surrounded by the Morse code messages with which the secret network talk to one another; in the next, he tracks their encrypted radio transmissions to the chamber of intoxication in which the transmitter is located, the opium den named 'The Blue Lotus'. On his way there he is drugged, 'buried' at sea again, woken up and reunited with his radio: the whole sequence of the two-book adventure is burial, transmission, burial, transmission. At one point he even transmits from his own grave (and incidentally, the fact that Snowy listens down the speaking-tube that pokes out from the earth calls to mind the HMV logo: the dog listening to 'His Master's Voice' emerging from a box which was originally represented as a coffin). In *The Black Island* Tintin again transmits from a place of death, Ben Mor or *mort* – a place which is also, according to Thompson and Thomson, guarded by ghosts – using a secret transmitter.

Abraham and Torok's crypt is the site of an encrypted trauma – and trauma, as Freud and his more empirically minded counterparts utterly agree if they agree on nothing else, instils in those unfortunate enough to undergo it a desire for repetition mixed with a need to disguise the scene being repeated. The crypt's emissions, accordingly, both reveal and re-encrypt: a double-move. Look at the magnificent visions Tintin has when doped with noxious fumes inside the Pharaoh's tomb: the burial, the reversion to Ur-time, the 'parents' and their pleasure, the removal of the child, the baby crying for comfort. It would be hard to find a better visual example of what Freud calls a 'primal scene', an original traumatic moment. But it is a primal scene that has been scrambled even as it plays itself out. Tintin's mind is doing here what Tintin does throughout the *oeuvre*: both uncovering and hiding. He will repeat this double-gesture later with Sir Francis Haddock's treasure and still later with the sun, ordering it to eclipse itself even as he looks it straight in the face.

Beneath what for Abraham and Torok is the almost-fictional character Sergei Pankajev, then, lies a story of 'the taboo-forming experience of a catastrophe, and finally beneath the catastrophe, the perennial memory of a hoarded pleasure with the ineducable wish that one day it will return'. This experience, this memory and this desire have given birth to a secret speech whose words, often transposed into images, acquire the status of coveted objects. As Abraham and Torok are at pains to point out, cryptonyms *themselves* become objects of desire: not content with simply *describing* the trauma-pleasure 'fetish', they become fetishes themselves. The process of transmitting them creates its own demented pleasure, becoming as compulsive as the need to paint Kih-Oskh signs over the trees of a whole forest. Through their reiteration, cryptonyms become 'generators of a situation that must be avoided and voided retroactively'. This is the pattern set by the crypt, pulsed out in its coded broadcasts. And this is the pattern of the *Tintin* books, their rhythms, their pulsing repetitions, their retroactive 'looking for noon at two o'clock' logic – not to mention their very cartoon medium itself, a hybrid in which words and images spill into and out of one another, birds encrypt names and opera titles birds, speech bubbles ooze from people's mouths but remain silent. This, too, is another truth of Thompson and Thomson in the desert, endlessly repeating a pattern whose originators they do not even recognise themselves to be.

For Abraham and Torok, Sergei Pankajev, or 'SP', has one extra-special word that, among all his crackling ones, does not speak at all: the *truly* silent word is *tieret*, Russian for rub, grind, scrape, wound. This threads through a dreamt skyscraper (*Wolkenkratzer* in German) to *Volk*, Russian for wolf, and on through Grusha rubbing the floor, the Tierek River,

Teresa (*Tieretsa* in Russian), ripping (*tierebit*) the wasp's wings off and a host of other scenes. Not only does *Tieret* bind sexual pleasure, fear and death together in a cryptonymic network, but it also stands for the process of marking and erasing through which SP's crypt, like RG's, is itself generated and maintained. This ultra-secret word is so potent, Abraham and Torok conclude, that it and it alone becomes the object of his love. To keep it safe he buries it inside his crypt and carries it around for all his life, showing and hiding it, saying it without saying it, 'repeating tirelessly to one and all, especially to his analyst: "Here is nothing" – in French, *rien, Tintin* – "hold it tight."'

iv

Okay, then, you might ask: *whose* crypt are we breaching in the *Tintin* books? Haddock's, in which case the original catastrophe is his ancestor Sir Francis's abandonment and non-recognition (and the hoarded pleasure that of Sir Francis's mother in Louis XIV's arms)? It is more dispersed than that: Thompson and Thomson, Calculus and Tintin himself move to its rhythms just as much as Haddock – as indeed do Jolyon Wagg, the Blackfoot Indians, the Emir and pretty much all the minor characters. Hergé's own, then, in which case the catastrophe is the non-recognition and abandonment of Léon and Alexis, the pleasure Marie Dewigne's? Tisseron, effectively, opts for the second answer, and sets about presenting the *Tintin oeuvre* as Hergé's digging up and reconstructing of his own troubled prehistory, his two o'clock search for his own noon. Calling to witness an extensive body of psychological research that shows how trauma transmits down families through several generations (fascinatingly, children will show symptoms of their parents' and grandparents' traumas even when they are ignorant of them), Tisseron cites Haddock's anger and alcoholism, Calculus's wilful deafness and Thompson and Thomson's inability to navigate the world of signs as tell-tale symptoms of this complex. He presents the name-switch from Georges Remi to Hergé as an encrypted reversal of the 'lie' the name Remi was in the first place, and Haddock's refound nobility as a wishful restitution of the family status. He is particularly good at hearing the word *kar* (Syldavian for 'King') repeat itself again and again: *Karaboudjan, Huascar, Carreidas, Picaros, Ottokar, Rascar Kapac* and so on, pulsing through the *oeuvre* 'like the memory of a royal presence' – or, he might have said, a magic word.

Tisseron may not be completely 'wrong'. But there are two problems with his approach. One is that the structure of the crypt is bigger than the structure of the family. It was in the work before it – the ghost-gramophone sequence in *Tintin in the Land of the Soviets* contains all the same elements ('ghosts', transmission, burial, treasure, even the spectre of cannibalism) as the ghost–ancestor–parrot scene in *Red Rackham's Treasure* – and it keeps pulsing out its rhythms long after the family saga has sunk so far from view that it is not even operating allegorically any more. Tintin floats in a sea awash with coded transmissions in *The Red Sea Sharks* just as he does in *Cigars of the Pharaoh* – but in the later work the crypt has become that of mid-twentieth-century history, whose traumas are not exclusive to Hergé. When Thompson and Thomson creep around the generating room of *Destination Moon*, terrified by the ghostly skeletons they fail to recognise as their own X-ray images, the crypt has become technology itself.

In the next book the main characters visit what Tintin calls 'a place of death', the surface of the moon, travelling there in what they describe as a 'tomb', a 'flying coffin'. Radio messages shuttle back and forth: from rocket to moon-surface to ground control and back again, while baddies listen in. Here, too, time-zones are overlaid: Thompson and Thomson become inadvertent stowaways because they do not know the difference *between* noon and two o'clock, or rather 1.34 (the rocket's launch time) and 13.34 (the time that, unfamiliar with twenty-four-hour clocks, they understand to be the rocket's launch time). Here, too, the sun is intently scrutinised ('We have succeeded in making direct measurements of the constant of solar radiation, and fixing exactly the limits of the solar spectrum in the ultra-violet,' Calculus writes in his logbook) then eclipses itself ('The sun has completely vanished,' Tintin reports as the lunar night falls). Here, too, is abandonment – or, rather, would-be abandonment by the aristocratic Jorgen of Haddock, Calculus and the detectives on the surface of the moon, thwarted by Tintin interrupting what he describes as 'a family squabble'. But are we to interpret all of this as no more than autobiographical code or shorthand? Is it not also about science, ethics, the creative process?

And what of the still later *Flight 714*, with all its simultaneity, its bats and monitors that seem to have 'escaped from the Ice Age' rubbing shoulders with radars and retractable-winged jets, its Second World War bunkers and ancient, cipher-covered caverns side by side, psychic transmissions emanating from the latter mediating between humans and the aliens who are 'passing by'? Is this simply cryptic autobiography as well? Is it not also about nature, corruption, our condition on the planet and in time? The book begins and ends in an airport, as Hergé intended an entire *Tintin* adventure he never got round to writing to take place in one. Is he not beginning to hint that, as the German poet Goethe put it, we are all aliens, 'guests on this dark earth'?

Which brings us to the second problem. Reading through to any fixed situation not only eliminates all the other ones that are implied, but also, more fundamentally, misses the constant reinfection going on within the work, *as* the work, the logic of its fraught pleasure. As the *Tintin* books develop, patterns repeat, 'carried' by different contexts, and as they do this they mutate, like a potent virus that gathers its own momentum as it spreads. Abraham and Torok point out that cryptonyms do not simply 'describe' a secret fetish; they become the fetish themselves, demanding their own repetition. If Hergé's *oeuvre* contains cryptic mechanisms, this does not mean that it simply hides something so that it can be discovered, but rather that it keeps forming crypts. If Tintin busts one gang, finds one transmitter, the crypt just relocates and starts transmitting elsewhere: South America, Scotland, Central Europe, a model ship, space. We should learn something from this. What? That when explored, the work will not explain the 'psychology' of Captain Haddock, Tintin, Thompson and Thomson, Calculus or Hergé. Rather, through a fantastically dynamic set of overlayerings and cross-encodings, it pulses out sequences that resonate at levels far beyond that of any individual, re-encrypting themselves even as they speak.

The crypt underwrites a creative process, not an analytical one. It is on the side of the pathology, not the cure. Hergé went to see a shrink in the late fifties when he started having dreadful dreams of endless white expanses. The shrink told him to stop writing. He stopped seeing the shrink, and started the white-expanse-filled *Tintin in Tibet*. What is *really* interesting about the cipher RG buried in his name is not so much the relation it bears to a specific family history as the way it acts out the manoeuvre that lies behind the *oeuvre*: the crypt's double-move of marking and erasure opens up the space of the work itself. Its retroactive movements become those of writing – and of reading. First comes the crypt, then comes the possibility of putting a body in or assigning a body to it. Inserting a body in the crypt is, of course, the strategy of Tintin's enemies, who keep trying to wall him and others up; the Egyptologists who become victims of this strategy in *The Cigars of the Pharaoh* should serve as a warning to readers – and not just of Hergé's work – of the dangers of mummification through interpretation. The wonderful thing about Tintin is that, no matter how many times the villains may try to enclose him in the tomb, wrap him up, strait-jacket him, he always escapes – and, having escaped, comes back for more and then escapes again. Nor does he, like Sarcophagus daubing Kih-Oskh signs with his paintbrush, morosely repeat the same cipher: he carries it elsewhere so that it can mutate and repeat itself in a more advanced form, again and again.

Tintin always escapes. He has to, because his radio awaits him; he has to reabsorb the next wave of transmissions. Each time he escapes, the writing escapes with him – and when the writing does, so should a good reading. Tintin (a 'journalist') is aware he will be read. He even leaves a message on the surface of the moon 'for those who may one day follow in our steps'. He will also be aware, as a radio operator, that the waves which carry his transmissions will travel outwards endlessly through space. Who knows where the signals will end up, or what they will end up meaning?

4

CASTAFIORE'S CLIT

Farinelli, the castrato (née Carlo Bruschi, 1705–82) by
Bartolomeo Nazari.

i

Balzac's Sarrasine falls in love with an opera singer. The first time he hears her, in the Teatro Argentina in Rome, he cries out involuntarily and is seized by an urge to charge onto the stage. He is so overwhelmed that he rises from his seat and, leaving the theatre, goes and leans against a pillar for support. 'He had,' writes Balzac, 'experienced such pleasure, or perhaps he had suffered so keenly, that his life had drained away like water from a broken vase.' Returning home, he starts drawing her from memory – again and again, frenziedly – then sculpting her. The next day he rents a box beside the stage for the whole season. After a few nights she notices him; contact is made via an intermediary, and the mechanisms are set in place that will lead to Sarrasine's downfall, turning him into both public fool and sacrificial cow.

La Zambinella sings Jommelli. La Castafiore sings Gounod. When Haddock hears her, in the Hippodrome in *The Seven Crystal Balls*, the dog in his box starts howling, and he has to leave his seat. Weakened, he leans against a pillar, which gives way, catapulting a cow-head onto his own and shocking him into charging onto the stage, humiliating himself (he ends up trapped in a broken kettle-drum). This is not the first time he has heard her: it is the sixteenth consecutive night. Like Sarrasine, he has heard her once and rented a box beside the stage for the whole season. But here the comparisons must end because, unlike Sarrasine, Haddock is not fixated by the opera singer but rather by another act on the same bill, a conjuror whose water-into-wine (not whisky, as the English translation has it) trick he has been imitating frenziedly at home for days. He has become entranced by, caught up in, an act of prestidigitation. Let's believe this for now.

What precisely does la Zambinella sing? We are not told. It could be *Dido Abandonnata*, Jommelli's 1747 opera about a heroine seduced then deserted by the noble Aeneas who was passing by on his way home from Troy. We know what la Castafiore sings: the Jewel Song from *Faust*. In the second act of Gounod's 1872 opera, Faust and his satanic accomplice Mephistopheles creep into the pretty young Margarita's garden and, while Mephistopheles, Oliveira da Figueira-like, distracts the neighbour, Faust woos her. Mephistopheles has used his supernatural skills not only to make the old Faust look young, but also to conjure up out of thin air a box of magnificent jewels which far outshine the flowers a rival suitor has left her. As the lowly Margarita holds them to her neck, she sings: *Ah! je ris de me voir si belle en ce miroir* . . . – 'Ah, I laugh to see myself so beautiful in this mirror.' 'Was I ever Margarita?' she asks. 'No,' she declares, 'this is not my face: it is the daughter of a king' – *la fille d'un roi*. Although she at first resists Faust's advances, after reappearing at her window above the garden she succumbs. She becomes pregnant, is accused of murdering the child, goes mad and is eventually executed, to be gathered up by angels.

Castafiore sings this song and nothing else. Despite reports that she will perform or has performed Rossini, Puccini and Verdi, the only number she does in the books is Gounod's. She sings about jewels and her admirers give her jewels. What are jewels? Symbols of affection, to be sure – but ones with an edge of looseness, danger. Jewels carry propositions: men buy them for women they want to bed but not necessarily wed. Hergé seems to like jewels: he scatters them liberally through the *Tintin* books. In the Congo there is a diamond racket which wreaks terror on the natives. *The Broken Ear* revolves around a sacred diamond, one that protects against poison; its theft represents a broken contract, violation, and brings slaughter. In *The Secret of the Unicorn–Red Rackham's Treasure* jewels are the legacy of a pirate's philandering and also involve slaughter (twice: the slaughter Rackham wrought to obtain them and that which Sir Francis wrought on him and his crew to relieve them of the jewels). In the present tense of that adventure they end up underpinning the lifestyle Haddock and his entourage will enjoy from now on.

In the next adventure, *The Seven Crystal Balls–Prisoners of the Sun*, jewels are also tied up in a back-story story of phil-andering. They are also sacred. But despite being heaped on Tintin, Haddock and Calculus at the adventure's end, they do not buoy up a lifestyle: the last jewels did that quite ade-quately. These new ones are given as Tintin and the Captain swear not to divulge the whereabouts or even existence of the

Temple of the Sun. Effectively, they are a bribe, a pay-off. If, realising this, we look back to the last story, we will see that this is what they ended up being there as well: a substitution for a revelation, for disclosure. And this, in turn, might lead us to suspect that the deeper truth of jewels throughout the *Tintin* books is this: that they keep a secret.

ii

Castafiore has a voice, and then some. Her voice can blow away all other discourse, as it does when she unleashes it during the trial scene in *Tintin and the Picaros*, or it can provide a cover for another conversation to take place beneath, as it does in the same book when Tintin plays it loudly on the surveilled hotel room's gramophone so that the bugs will not pick up what Pablo has to tell him. Either way, it follows Tintin and Haddock everywhere, from Wadesdah to the mountains of Tibet. People love it – the crowds at La Scala cry for more – and they hate it. 'Silence! Silence! Silence!' screams the Los Dopicos prosecutor as his lawyers tremble under its onslaught. The very musicians who accompany her in Klow grimace in anguish as it washes over them; even the microphone strains away from it.

What does it tell? A story of sex, violation, pleasure, shame, a lost child, madness, condemnation. In Bianca Castafiore the crypt's emanations, its transmissions and its rhythms are embodied in a single character. She is, as Haddock calls her, catastrophe, and she is not just the hope that it will return but also the return itself, its triumphant self-assertion, its encore. Through her the primal scene – Haddock's, Hergé's, everyone's and no one's – is transposed into a myth and, amplified, repeated: again and again and again.

Let's track her through the books. She first appears in *King Ottokar's Sceptre*, where Tintin meets her in the Auberge de la Couronne, 'The Crown Inn' (the vital royal association is lost in the English substitution of 'The Coachman's Rest'). Here he upgrades from the Syldavian peasant's cart in which he has previously been riding to her car. In the forest just beyond the Inn, the cart is held up by anti-monarchist conspirators who demand to know where Tintin is. The peasant has a stammer and does not manage to tell them that he is in the approaching car before, hearing its engine, the conspirators hide behind a rock, leaving the peasant to mutely point at it as it speeds by. 'Th-th-the y-y-young f-f-f-for-foreigner w-w-W-wwas in . . . in . . . in th-th-that c-c-car w-w-w-which j-j-just papa-papa-passed!' he eventually stammers when they return. It is as though language, like the microphone, were shying away from the message it is carrying. Tongue cannot speak and ear cannot hear: Tintin, like Haddock in the theatre, abandons his seat in the car when Castafiore sings for him, claiming to have left something at the Inn. 'I would have given any excuse to escape!' he says. He will interrupt her performance again the next evening, a performance for the King himself, to warn him of the imminent theft of his sceptre, but language again fails him as Jorgen and his accomplices gag him. The next morning the sceptre is stolen, threatening a total loss of the King's power.

Look at the conspirator who holds up the cart: Haddock has not been created yet, but this man has Haddock's face, his beard, his expression. He is Haddock *avant la lettre*. Look at the bearded guardians of the Royal Treasure Chamber: proto-Haddocks too, all of them. Haddock is born in the next adventure, *The Crab with the Golden Claws*, but it is in this one that he is gestated, from the moment Papa pa-pa-passes by. With Castafiore's next appearance, in the *Sarrasine*-like music-hall scene of *The Seven Crystal Balls* (and despite the English version's jigging to accommodate the fact that this book was translated after *The Red Sea Sharks* and *The Calculus Affair*), Haddock is seeing her for the first time – or rather we are seeing him see her for the first time: he has been in the same box for sixteen nights. But the retroactive movement that fires through the books on all channels dictates that he has encountered her in the forest of an earlier, primal stage of his development – and also that the story of seduction, violation and non-recognition which she sings sums up and repeats his own. That he becomes obsessed by the water-into-wine trick a couple of numbers down the bill – or, as Michel Serres would say, two links down the chain – is a piece of prestidigitation to the power of two, a sleight of hand hidden in a sleight of hand. It is by Castafiore that Haddock is *really* captivated. He will, like Sarrasine, imitate her self-consciously in *Destination Moon*, playing the control room's instrument panel like a piano as he sings *Ah! je ris de me voir si belle en ce miroir* . . . before losing his own mini-sceptre, his pipe; here at the opera, though, he plays his fascination with her out at an even deeper level, frantically repeating their encounter while disguising this fact even from himself.

The encounter replays for him in a literal way with Castafiore's next appearance five books later, in *The Calculus Affair*. Again Haddock, Tintin and Snowy sit in a theatre and listen to her sing (with Snowy's jaw bound this time, as Tintin's was in Klow). Again they wander backstage, where Haddock is actually introduced to her for the first time, or rather introduces himself when she asks 'this fisherman's' name. 'Er . . . Hoddack . . . er . . . Had-dad . . . Excuse me, Haddock,' he replies, as language breaks down yet again. This time Sponsz, not Ottokar, will lose his power, have his treasure chamber violated; out of it will come Calculus, the deaf man who has invented the sound weapon that fractures Haddock's image in the mirror at the story's outset, leaving him neither beautiful nor laughing, and, echoing a metaphor from *Sarrasine*, breaks his vases ('Had a tiff with the wife?' asks Jolyon Wagg when he sees the shattered fragments).

The relations here are complex, to say the least. But they all turn around a certain violence of articulation or its threat (in French, incidentally, the word for 'blackmail' is *chantage*, 'singing'). We have known since Haddock sneezed in the snow-laden Andes in *Prisoners of the Sun* that sound is dangerous and can bring mountains crashing down. But what we might have forgotten is that Castafiore's voice was presented as a weapon from her first entry in *King Ottokar's Sceptre*. 'It's lucky the windows are strong!' murmurs Tintin, looking at the safety glass as the words 'Was I ever Margarita!' half-shatter his eardrums in the car. Later, in *The Castafiore Emerald* (which we will look at in more detail in a moment), when Castafiore announces her imminent departure 'to South America to conquer the capitals', Haddock will silently add: 'And reduce them to ruins as well!' We should suspect another sleight of hand in *The Calculus Affair*'s city-destroying weapon. After all, the secret plans for it turn out to have been sitting at home the whole time, just like Red Rackham's jewels and the Sun King's secret.

So it is to 'home' that, after a walk-on part in *The Red Sea Sharks* ('What shall we do? . . . Hop back on the raft?' asks Haddock when Castafiore greets them in 'Art's' name as they are rescued from the sea) and a radio-slot in *Tintin in Tibet* ('can't a man get a moment's peace . . . anywhere?' the Captain wonders after hearing her on the sherpas' wireless), she comes for her next major appearance, in Hergé's masterpiece whose title bears her name, *The Castafiore Emerald*. Even the book's cover is a stroke of genius: in front of cameras and lights, Castafiore sings; Haddock covers his ears; Tintin, in the foreground, looks straight out at the reader holding his finger to his lips. When the cover scene is played out inside the book, Castafiore, in performing the Jewel Song in the Maritime Gallery, re-enacts Haddock's ancestral drama of seduction and abandonment in the room consecrated to his ancestor, in front of the fetish-like statue of the ancestor himself. The island natives whom Sir Francis befriended after blowing up the *Unicorn* have carved him with his mouth wide open, shouting something, yet the statue is, of course, silent.

No matter: she voices the message he could not deliver, and voices it loud and clear for everyone to hear. Each time she is interrupted (count them: three times) she just starts again.

As Freud knows all too well, whatever is suppressed repeats. Haddock suppresses the hand-biting episode from his account to Miarka's family of his encounter with the gypsy child and so the episode repeats, again and again: the parrot bites him twice and a bee stings him for good measure. The repetition in *The Castafiore Emerald* is obsessive. The whole book runs on its loops: falling down the stairs, phoning Bolt the builder, scales, scales, scales. It runs with the regularity of a machine – so much so that parts of it can be replaced by a cassette and the character can take a break, wander offstage. There is a huge self-consciousness about it: 'MERCY! MY JEWELS!' 'There she goes! . . . She's lost her geegaws again.' 'MURDER!' 'You hear?' 'Yes, yes . . . don't worry: she'll find them in a minute or two.' 'MY EMERALD!' '*THUMP*' 'Someone's missed that step again.' Those who can discern the rhythms can step into them and operate in their blind spots: Wagner, the photographer, the magpie . . .

Calculus understands nothing of the mechanism, trips over its wires. This, of course, is also sleight of hand: in fact, he understands everything only too well. He may not be able to hear Castafiore sing, or even know that she is a singer, but he is tuned in to a more fundamental stratum of the story, a subsonic frequency. 'Professor, you make me blush!' she exclaims as he kisses her hand and compliments her on 'the boldness of the colour' in the paintings for which he believes she is famous. In the original French, she tells him: *vous me faites rougir!*, 'you make me become red'. Calculus will spend the next few days in his garden 'raising a completely new variety of rose': a white one, 'pearly, sparkling, immaculate'. Its name? *Bianca*, 'white': *Bianca Castafiore*. Via her name, he whitens her; turns her from a deflowered woman back into a chaste rose. In his zone of near-silence, he injects language into a flower. And it is from a flower that it blooms, through a cross-pollination of information, into a Paris–Flash report. But the miswired conversation with the journalists, in which the secret of the rose becomes that of the wedding and the Chelsea Flower Show in which lie its origins the location of the lovers' meeting and so on, is not in fact miswired at all. It is constructed with a rocket scientist's skill for routing, plotting elliptical paths of departure and return. Why? Because, in leading to the 'revelation' of a hushed-up betrothal, it loops back to where the whole thing started: with a secret sexual union – but loops back there in such a way that it will not be recognised. Rerouted back to itself, the event will be misread. It is Thompson and Thomson in the desert all over again.

The Castafiore Emerald is endlessly regressive, endlessly overdetermined. It stacks up layers of meaning like so many pancakes, toy bricks, sheets of acetate: the layer of family secrets, the layer of mannerist comedy, the layer of media commentary, communications theory, social criticism, *et patati et patata* as the Captain says – and yet it simultaneously erases any referent. What is the book *about*? Who knows? Three books previously, in *The Calculus Affair*, hordes of people camp outside Marlinspike's gates to watch Calculus's sound weapon shatter Haddock's windows. This time the sound weapon is much more powerful, because much more is at stake. This time the media are let into the château itself, and via them the whole world is called to witness and to hear. And yet, as they were last time, they will be disappointed. Calculus, on his subsonic stratum, knows this too. In the whiteness of his rose, beyond the more obvious restitution of Bianca's purity, lurks a meaning that sends us the other way: the real trauma might be not defloration but its opposite: the 'white', unconsummated marriage (to a gardener, no less). This is also the catastrophe which the book replays, through the non-consummation of its event field. To put it really simply: nothing happens. No wonder the twins are upset. 'Why are they so cross? Oh dear, what have I done?' asks Castafiore. Nothing: that is the problem. For Thompson and Thomson, this trauma will repeat again when the 'thieves' turn out to be innocent.

The event field is unconsummated; and language fails to deliver – on its promises (marriage) and on its threats or *chantage* (revelation). That is what is so tantalising and so agonising about this book. And it is the truth behind the anguishing intensity of Castafiore's song. As the front cover all but shows us at the outset, the voice that carries the secret remains inaudible even as it is amplified – as inaudible, ultimately, as that of the statue. It may terrorise the heroes, burn their ears, but it stops short of destroying their world by naming the event *as* the event. In repeating the event otherwise, through fable and in song, it carries out a double-articulation that is also a counter-articulation, one that erases itself as it scores the surface of the air, silences even as it speaks. 'Now, signora, just a few words from you please,' the television sound man asks; 'Er . . . my turn now? . . . Just a few words? . . . Well . . . I . . . I . . . I'm happy . . . so very . . . happy . . . Well, I don't really know how to put it . . . Ah! ha! ha!' Castafiore responds. She speaks in order to say nothing.

The event field is unconsummated. Speech says nothing. And, of course, this provides the blind spot for the event to happen in, for everything to be said.

iii

Bianca Castafiore has been 'engaged' by the newspapers to many men: the Maharaja of Gopal, Baron Halmaszout, the Lord Chamberlain of Syldavia, Colonel Sponsz and the Marquis di Gorgonzola (alias Rastapopoulos). Has she fucked them? Hergé would spend ages discussing the lives of his characters with his assistants, and must have thought so at some level. But at what level? We would have to go 'beyond' the page to find out, or at least behind the scenes – and then of course the story would not exist any more, or at least not in the same way. Haddock and Tintin go behind the scenes in *The Seven Crystal Balls*, and walk into another story, that of the Sun God's curse – that is, they walk into another section of the same larger story. But when they go backstage again in *The*

Calculus Affair, at the opera in Szohôd, they find Castafiore herself in the dressing room, as we have already seen. When Sponsz, who is hunting them down, turns up there too, they go behind the scenes of the behind-scene scene, hiding among clothes in a curtained-off wardrobe. What do they see from there?

Castafiore has just performed Gounod's *Faust*, 'sublime' (as one of the secret police stooges puts it) in the role of Margarita. Backstage, she may be out of character, but she has 'put on Margarita's prettiest gown' to receive 'my admirers', of whom Sponsz is the most powerful. 'I am deeply honoured, Ma'am to . . . to find myself in the presence of the celebrated singer who . . . er . . . who . . .' he stammers. 'Fie, Colonel!' she replies. 'You make me blush!' – *rougir* again. She proposes champagne. 'Come, Colonel, make yourself useful,' she tells him. 'You may open the bottle.' As he is suavely edging its cork out two soldiers enter, looking for Tintin and Haddock. 'You dunderheaded nitwits!' he shouts at them. 'Go on, get out! About turn, before I explode!' In doing this, Sponsz falls for a double-chamber trick himself, sending two 'dummy' witnesses away but failing to notice the real ones lurking in the enclave right beside him. Tintin and Haddock listen as he tells Castafiore all about his kidnapping of Calculus and his plans to release him to the Red Cross only if he divulges the secret of the sound weapon and signs a declaration that he came to Borduria of his own free will. The scene is ridiculous and totally implausible – unless we interpret it as pillow talk, or as like the scenes in David Lynch's 1986 film *Blue Velvet* (which, incidentally, opens with a severed ear) in which the hero, peeping from a closet, watches the crazed villain Frank writhe in sexual excitement in front of his singer victim as he moans out his deranged visions of power. Then it makes complete sense. Sponsz, like Frank, is spilling his psychotic dreams – and spilling them a little too fast. As he points the soldiers to the door, warning them that he is about to explode, he loses his grip on the champagne bottle and pops his cork prematurely.

Here is a perfect example of the 'most active figural capacity' of objects in cartoons: an image playing out a vulgar expression and setting up a sexual channel of communication which operates alongside the literal one. Tisseron finds instances of this throughout the books: in Haddock's continual breaking of his pipe in *Destination Moon,* in the multiple mast-breaking of *Secret of the Unicorn* (*casser la pipe* and *casser la mâte* both mean 'to be castrated'). Following this logic, we could see in the plaster-covered leg that sticks straight out in front of Haddock in *The Castafiore Emerald* a sign of both castration and an erection. We could see an erection in his red and swollen finger which Castafiore holds up and inspects, and another in his red and swollen nose from which she extracts a big prick. These would not be mere projections on our part: Hergé, like all good Catholic boys, has a filthy mind. He delights in cranking up the vulgar channel to its max. Look at Ramón returning to his and Alonso's hotel room in *The Broken Ear* with a bullet in his buttock. 'Oooh! . . . He keell me! . . . Ooooh!' he moans, before sitting on Alonso's needle-stuffed pincushion. *You like pricks in your butt, fag?* Hergé is mocking him; *Here, have some more. And more*: as Ramón lies in bed later with his sore buttocks sticking up, Alonso reads him a newspaper report about a corporal 'wounded by a cactus spine'. As a fun exercise, try to do a 'vulgar' scan of the whole *oeuvre*. You will pick up on the scenes in *The Crab with the Golden Claws* where Haddock, delirious from dehydration, pictures Tintin as a bottle of champagne ready to gush and Tintin, himself dreaming that he has been trapped inside a bottle, screams as the Captain, wielding a giant corkscrew, penetrates and screws him. You will raise your eyebrows as you watch the torpedo-nose of the shark-submarine driven by Tintin plunge between the Captain's buttocks and thrust outwards from his crotch in *Red Rackham's Treasure*. You will do a double-take when you realise that the diagram above Calculus's head in the factory in *Destination Moon* depicts the twin cheeks of a bottom. And much, much more.

Which loops us back to a question a version of which we have posed already: what is Castafiore's emerald? Viewed with the sexual sub-filter 'on', the answer will not be long in coming. She sits on it. It is hard to find, and easy to lose again among the moundy grass, tucked away in its nest or under folds of cushion. It was given to her for pleasure, for the pleasure she gives to men; it gives her pleasure and encourages her to give men more pleasure. It is a clitoris, duh. In the privacy of her bedroom she removes it from its box, looks at it, touches it, sings, transported: *Ah, ah, aaaaah je ris* . . .

It is a clitoris – and then of course it is not: it is an emerald, given to her by a Maharaja. Barthes, pondering Sarrasine's actions when he hears la Zambinella, shows how the involuntary cries, the image of spillage and the subsequent evenings during which the sculptor, lying on a sofa in his box, 'created for himself a pleasure as rich and varied as he wished it to be' could be taken to mean *he ejaculates when he hears her, then returns and masturbates to her voice every night*, or could simply be taken to mean *he is enchanted when he hears her, and returns to hear her more*. Or rather, Barthes shows how they simultaneously mean both: the 'literal' is just one code operating alongside the figural. Meaning is (as they say of erections) 'achieved' when both codes are up and running, when there is a coupling of systems. The question, for the reader, becomes one of negotiating these. For Tisseron, Thompson and Thomson, who make figures of speech literal via their pendulum readings in *Prisoners of the Sun*, are exemplary bad readers, the type of person who thinks *casser la pipe* means to break a pipe rather than to be castrated. But they merely do what Tintin himself does with the opera title *La Gazza Ladra*: read from the figure to the world. Maybe Thompson and Thomson are double-bluffs, and represent instead the critic who thinks *casser la pipe* means having your penis chopped off. Then again, Red Rackham's treasure is located in the map, not the world: what do we make of that? And even then, how are we to understand its jewels? As clitorises too?

Calculus reads from world to figure: he thinks the Inca temple at the end of *Prisoners of the Sun* is a stage set. He is both wrong and right: within the book's plot it is a real Inca temple, and within the *oeuvre's* wider symbolic context it is a figural construction, a transposition of another situation (that of Louis and Sir Francis). While Haddock looks for his pipe in the control room of *Destination Moon,* arse sticking out from under the table, Calculus corrects, and corrects his corrections. He seems to intuit the fact that objects and situations are caught up in a chain of substitutions that keeps moving. If the diamond in *The Broken Ear* is a clitoris, it is a metaphorical one, the 'clitoris' of the Arumbaya tribe, their pleasure, wrapped up in a fetish. It is also a counterpart for the Gran Chapo oil which the companies, those other western visitors or passers-by, want to plunder: a rich, secret thing hiding in the dark, in the earth's folds and pleats, desired by many men – and also, like Red Rackham's jewels, calling for slaughter, in this case the technologised slaughter of modern war. It is also a symbol of value: monetary value for Alonso and Ramón, hermeneutic value for Tintin (it solves the mystery of why people want the fetish). And on top of all that, it is stolen by the interpreter. If, as Serres says, the excess of language steals the jewel in *The Castafiore Emerald,* then in *The Broken Ear* it is the movement between languages that does it: the jewel is lost in translation. This is the event, the trauma that repeats at the end of this book: as Ramón, Alonso and Tintin all grab at it, the diamond slips away, like Calculus's trial rocket.

Sarrasine sees la Zambinella and sees perfection. She has 'the ideal beauty he had hitherto sought in life'; in her face and body are displayed 'all the wonders of those images of Venus revered by the chisels of the Greeks'. He makes a sculpture of her and hopes that this will be a prelude to possessing her himself, that, like Pygmalion, he can move from the statue to the thing behind or inside it. But as it progresses, Balzac's text, like Hergé's, starts correcting itself. Doubt is thrown on the status and nature of la Zambinella. Lines such as 'And if I were not a woman?' posed to the sculptor by la Zambinella 'in a soft silvery voice', plus the fact that her side-kicks are always whispering and smiling, lead us to suspect that 'she' might in fact be a man, and that the flowing skirts concealing her body from him might actually conceal a penis. This, though, turns out to be a bad correction. What we find out at the end is that la Zambinella is neither a man nor a woman but a castrato, an eighteenth-century phenomenon that sent audiences wild all over Europe, sang gala perform-ances for kings, made fortunes, and were as renowned for their capriciousness as for their talent. What the veils were hiding was not something but rather the fact of nothing: an absence, a hollow, a void.

La Zambinella's castration is radical. It not only precludes all pleasure (his, 'hers') but also oozes through the text, infect-ing everything, emptying out all value. 'To love, to be loved are henceforth meaningless words for me, as they are for you,' cries Sarrasine when he discovers the truth; 'I shall forever think of this imaginary woman when I see a real woman.' The narrator who tells the story to Mme de Rochefide is not going to get off either: his prey, genuinely shocked by the story she has heard, renounces sex for life. Castration becomes much more than just a physical fact or psychological condition: it overtakes the whole symbolic order and becomes its truth. As Barthes puts it: 'the contagious force of castration explodes'. Morphology, grammar and discourse are transgressed; mean-ing is abolished; 'language dies'.

For Barthes, the character Sarrasine is an allegory of the

realist artist or writer, and of the whole realist mode. Why? Firstly because he does not realise that what he thought was 'real' was in fact only a transcription of a set of cultural codes ('images of Venus . . . chisels of the Greeks'), just as a 'realist' reading of the Sarrasine-in-box (or Sponsz-with-cork) passage is merely 'a transcription of the literality of the symbol'. Secondly, and more fundamentally, because he wants the thing inside the image, inside language, without realising that inside is emptiness. At another, more intuitive level, of course, he realises this: on this level he wants castration itself because it is the secret truth of art, and goes back and back to hear la Zambinella's voice because he is fixated and infected with this secret. What he is tuning into, hearing everywhere he goes, unable to escape from, is castration's frequency, its whispering, its laughter.

As Sarrasine, Haddock. Castafiore's voice draws him behind the realistic surface of things into a hollow world where landscape has no depth, where bars are only figural and collapse, where columns hold nothing up (cities do come crashing down, but only fake ones). This stage set sacrifices him on its hollow altar, leaving him trapped inside an empty, perforated drum. Naming him, her voice removes his name: she calls him Bartok, Karbock, Kapstock, even Balzac, but never Haddock. Drawing him into the machinations of the media – that is, of public, social 'language' – it ensnares him in a ritual of fullness that has no substance behind it, of fulfilment that gives no satisfaction, 'love' without love. Echoing Sarrasine's line 'To love, to be loved are henceforth meaningless words for me, as they are for you,' she waves away the

Captain's indignation at reports of their impending wedding with the words: 'But it doesn't mean a thing.'

Hergé treats his capricious megastar who announces herself as 'Art' to the same language as that to which Balzac treats la Zambinella. 'A celestial harpy', Sarrasine calls her; 'siren with a serpent's heart . . . gorgon with a voice of gold,' the Los Dopicos prosecutor calls la Castafiore. Sarrasine complains that she has 'thrust her talons into all my manly feelings'; Haddock dreams in *Tintin and Alph-Art* of a giant bird-like Castafiore pecking at him as she digs her claws into his body. 'A woman . . . or should we call her a monster?' asks the prosecutor. It is true that she looks less and less like a woman as the books progress. To interpret something literal from that (that she is actually a transsexual, for example) would be as futile as to declare that she 'definitely' does or does not have sex with Sponsz, the Maharaja or the Baron. What is certain, though, is that castration unfolds around her, from her: not the trivial, coy, punning one of broken pipes or masts but of figuration in its entirety, the ability of things to mean, of language and the world to correspond, of signs to have some content. Standing at her bedroom window in *The Castafiore Emerald* after she is disturbed by something during her first night in Marlinspike – her bedroom window which, like Margarita's, overlooks the garden – Tintin stares out into pure blackness and announces, in one of the most brilliant single frames in the whole *oeuvre*: 'There's nothing here, signora. Absolutely nothing.'

As Sarrasine, Haddock, and as Haddock the whole universe of the *Tintin* books. To borrow Barthes's line, the contagious force of castration explodes. *The Castafiore Emerald* is the ground zero of its detonation, but its ripples reach out everywhere, right to the *oeuvre's* beginning. They reach back to the factory façade and fake elections in the Soviet Union, to the hollowing out of fetishes and belief in the Congo, and from the slaughtering and packaging of cows in America right to the carving up, emptying out and hanging in shop windows of language itself in the name of art in the final, uncompleted book. Castafiore turns up in that one too, and hails Alph-Art as *un véritable rétour aux sources*, a return to the origins of art. Perhaps she is not wrong.

This principle of negation, of the non-event, of meaning's cancellation: 'Cataclysm! Calamity! Catastrophe!' – castration. Haddock may not say this last word when he receives the telegram informing him that Castafiore is coming, but Calculus hears it anyhow. It is another meaning hoarded up, held in reserve in his flower trick: under the name of Bianca, he genetically mutates or genitally mutilates a rose so as to bypass its normal reproductive processes. Two books later, in *Tintin and the Picaros*, castration will make a species leap from flowers to people: with pills derived from 'medicinal herbs' which induce an aversion to alcohol in those who unwittingly swallow them, Calculus will remove all bacchanalian pleasure from Haddock, from the Picaros and, most poignantly, from the Arumbayas whose diamond was first plundered and then slipped away to the depths of the earth's crust, unplumbable. The Gran Chapo, incidentally, turned out to have no oil in it – but what Calculus is saying with his rose, on the most subsonic frequency of all, is: Castafiore has no clit.

At the end of Balzac's novella, Sarrasine tries to smash his sculpture of la Zambinella, throwing a hammer at its perch but, like Ramón throwing his knife at the perched parrot, missing. He is then immediately killed by three men in the employ of the jealous and powerful Cardinal Cicognara, la Zambinella's protector, who rescue the sculpture at the same time. What really kills him, Barthes says, is the abolition of meaning he has just experienced. If he welcomes his murder as 'a good deed worthy of a Christian', this is because it returns him to the universe of fixed, absolute value. Ramón and Alonso are taken up by this universe as well at the end of *The Broken Ear*. The fetish they have pursued throughout the book, desperate to get at what is inside it, has just smashed and become hollow at the same moment. While they are led away by devils it, too, is rescued. Gathered up, it is pieced together and returned to the museum in which we first saw it, while its guardian sings opera in the background.

5

ADONIS AND HIS COUNTERFEIT

Fake *Mona Lisas* on display.

i

Let's start where we left off: the artist Sarrasine makes a sculpture, a copy of la Zambinella. While doing this, he is unable to see the mark of castration on her body. He is killed. Replace 'Sarrasine' with 'Balthazar' and you have got the core plot of *The Broken Ear*: the artist Balthazar makes a sculpture, a copy of an Arumbaya fetish. While doing this, he fails to notice the mark on its body, a chip in its ear (its genitals are covered by a kind of nappy). Balthazar is killed. What happens next?

Well, Sarrasine's sculpture is copied into marble by the Cardinal's (his killer's) men, and deposited in a museum. The de Lanty family, whose mother is la Zambinella's niece, have the artist Vien copy it as a painting: it becomes the Adonis which started the whole story off by sparking Mme de Rochefide's curiosity. Another painter, Girodet, then uses Vien's Adonis as the source for his own work depicting Endymion and the moon. Copies, copies, copies: what became of the original we do not find out.

Would the same find-and-replace exercise work here? Almost – but Hergé's plot is cleverer. After killing Balthazar, his murderer Tortilla places the copy he has commissioned from the sculptor back in the museum he robbed in the first place, passing it off as the original. But, unbeknown to him, Balthazar has made *two* copies, and passed one of them off to Tortilla as the original. Effectively, Tortilla plays the role of both the Cardinal (killing, having a copy made) *and* of Sarrasine, taking for an original what was in fact a fake. He, too, will be killed. And so, too, as we have seen, will his killers, who, like him, hope to make a fortune from what lies concealed in the fetish. Balthazar's brother, a commercial sculptor, finds the *real* original in his trunk after his death and, unaware of its provenance, has hundreds of copies of it made in his artisan-studios, selling these to secure, if not a fortune, then at least a moderate source of income.

Had Hergé read *Sarrasine* when he wrote *The Broken Ear*? Possibly. By *The Red Sea Sharks* the answer must be 'probably'. It is hard not to see in the stupendous ball on board the *Scheherazade* a reflection of the de Lantys' party, where 'milling about, whirling around, flitting here and there, were the most beautiful women in Paris, the richest, the noblest, dazzling, stately, resplendent with diamonds, flowers in their hair, on their bosoms, on their heads, strewn over dresses or in garlands at their feet', while a now-aged la Zambinella, who has the air of 'a kind of Faust', slinks among them ghoul-like. It is even harder not to hear in the gossip of the fancy-dressed guests of di Gorgonzola (who moves among them dressed as Faust) an echo of the de Lantys' revellers' chatter. 'Naturally, malicious tongues spread rumours that he has a shady past,' a monocled nobleman of Hergé's mutters to a pharaoh. 'Even if it's the devil,' says a politician of Balzac's, 'they give a marvellous party' – to which a philosopher ecstatically adds: 'Even if Count de Lanty had robbed a bank, I'd marry his daughter any time!'

'Nobody knew what country the de Lanty family came from, or from what business, what plunder, what piratical activity, or what inheritance derived a fortune estimated at several millions,' writes Balzac. The answer, of course, is that they come from Italy and that their fortune comes from a backstory of seduction, copying and murder – that is, it comes from la Zambinella, who amassed it during 'her' career as an opera singer – and it comes to them indirectly, 'sideways': 'she' could have no heirs. But these facts, even were they known, would not necessarily count against them in Paris, where (as Balzac's narrator quips) 'even bloodstained or filthy money betrays nothing and stands for everything'. Di Gorgonzola's money is bloodstained and filthy too: it comes from slavery. But while his guests in the floating Paris of the Red Sea may speculate on its source, they are not too concerned to get to the bottom of it as long as it keeps buying them champagne. Tintin, drinking sea-water, is concerned and does get to the bottom of it, rumbling di Gorgonzola's racket and exposing him as a fraud, a cover for Rastapopoulos.

Copying, imitating, 'passing off': these themes, which concern Hergé as much as Balzac, fall into place around the question of the provenance of money. And this provenance, for both, is tied in with interrupted or occluded family structures. For Hergé this develops slowly, over several books. In Russia we have fake factories and wealth-hoarding by the state (what the gramophone 'ghosts' guard is a secret bunker full of the treasures that Lenin, Trotsky and Stalin have stolen from the people), and in America fake policemen, imitation castles and banks that spring up overnight as wealth gushes from the ground to be hoarded by big business (the oil companies who kick the Blackfoot Indians off their territory so they can exploit it). If in *The Broken Ear* the act of forgery brings money putatively to the thief and the thief's robbers and actually to his brother, in the next book, *The Black Island* (which Hergé originally intended to call *Les Faux-Monnayeurs*, 'The Forgers'), it is the money itself that is fake, illegally printed on a secret press in Scotland. In the next one, *King Ottokar's Sceptre*, the brother is fake, robbing his twin Hector Alembick's identity as part of a plot to interrupt what the tourist brochure informs us is the already-interrupted line of royal ascendance in Syldavia. Then, on the trail of false money in *The Crab with the Golden Claws*, Tintin meets the complexly ancestored Haddock; soon, sloughing off the host of false descendants of Red Rackham who turn up on the Captain's doorstep waving spurious genealogical charts, they set out to recover stolen money and end up retrieving a lost inheritance in the process.

Let's look more closely at this money, and at money – and fake money – in general. The philosopher Jacques Derrida, in his 1991 book *Given Time: 1. Counterfeit Money*, turns to the etymological root of the word 'economy' and finds it has two parts: *oikos*, Greek for 'home', and *nomos*, Greek for 'law'. This second part, *nomos*, itself breaks down into the laws of distribution (*nemein*) and of partition (*moira*, which also means 'lot' or 'destiny'). Besides the values of law and home, of distribution and partition, economy also implies 'the idea of exchange, of circulation, or return'. Goods and products are exchanged and circulated, as is money itself, and in venturing money people hope that they will get at least as much back again, if not more. Pondering these facts, Derrida begins to suspect that 'the law of economy is the – circular – return to the point of departure, to the origin, also to the home'. Waxing mythical, he talks of the 'odyssean' nature of economy, suggesting that '*Oikonomeia* would always follow the path of Ulysses' – *Odysseus* and *Ulysses* being two names for the same Homeric hero whose destiny or *moira* dictated that he embark on a twenty-year-long adventure that would end with his return to his own palace.

The Odyssean circuit, the path of Ulysses: this is exactly Haddock's path, the loop he follows, his destiny. Born several generations after a partition was made and lots assigned (one ship to each son), and several-plus-one generations after another, cruel lot was handed out – a cruel lot which nonetheless left his ancestor richer to the tune of one stately home – Haddock sets out around the world in order to return to the point of departure, which is the home itself. The home that he returns to was not the one *he* left but rather that left by – and to – Sir Francis: his circuit is a trans-generational one. And it is money, the treasure, that sends him on this path that leads back to the home (the home whose butler, incidentally, has a name straight out of Homer's *Odyssey*: Nestor).

For Derrida, economy raises another question: the gift. As a phenomenon that also involves exchange and circulation, the gift is both tied to economic systems and a contradiction of these systems: giving is opposed to buying and selling; it is 'free'. On top of that, the language of the gift lies at the heart of our philosophical and general ideas, so much so that we take it for granted and hardly even notice it. To say something exists in German we say *Es gibt*, 'it gives': *Es gibt einen Mann*, 'there is a man', or, to quote the great philosopher Martin Heidegger, *Es gibt Sein*, 'there is being'. In English we say something or someone is 'present', and the horizon within which they exist is 'the present'. So fundamentally does the structure of giving underpin our categories of thought and of existence, Derrida concludes, that we cannot even properly say that one person or subject gives a gift to another subject: rather, 'subject and object are arrested effects of the gift, arrests of the gift' – freeze-frames, as it were, taken from the gift's fundamental movement, from 'the zero or infinite speed of the circle'.

What does the gift give? Time. Turning to the anthropologist Marcel Mauss, whose studies of Melanesian and Polynesian tribes form the basis of his 1950 book *The Gift: The Form and Reason for Exchange in Archaic Societies*, Derrida notices Mauss's observation that 'in every possible form of society, it is in the nature of a gift to impose an obligatory time limit or term'. A gift, says Mauss, *obliges* and, since the obligation cannot be acquitted or returned immediately (if it were, the gift would not be a gift but simply form part of a normal economic exchange), a delay is set in place, an interval of indebtedness. Gratitude is owed, and that debt must not be forgotten: it must be repaid before too long. Thus past and future tenses open up around the 'present' of the gift.

Haddock's time opens up with the gift: the gift from Louis XIV to Sir Francis of a château and the gift from Tintin to the Captain of the model ship that puts him onto it: a double, staggered gift, a gift within a gift. From Tintin's gift a whole past era unfolds, and the immediate future is devoted to looping back to catch up with that past and dig it up within the present. In the Caribbean, Haddock finds himself awash in time itself – twentieth-century time with its meridian set at Greenwich, seventeenth-century time with its meridian in Paris: noon and two o'clock overlaid even as Haddock and his entourage, to borrow Baudelaire's line again, look for noon at two o'clock.

For Derrida, though, neither Haddock's nor Mauss's gifts are proper gifts. According to him, a *real* gift should not impose conditions and indebtedness; it should be genuinely 'free'. But in order to function in this way, the gift would have to be unrecognisable as a gift, that is, it would have to cancel or annul itself, to undergo 'radical forgetting' – not just overlooking but an absolute erasure that places it outside of time itself. Otherwise, it is only a partial gift, one that, in obliging the recipient and making them owe, takes more than it gives. Normal gifts are 'bad' gifts, Derrida says; they are unhealthy. As Mauss himself points out, the Latin word for 'gift', *dosis*, is a transcription of the Greek *dosis*, 'dose of poison', just as the German word for poison is (wait for it) *Gift* – etymological and cross-linguistic links that lead Derrida to write of 'the poisoned gift of which legacies are made'.

The *Tintin* books are full of bad gifts, gifts which bring grief to the recipients, gifts which are poisonous. The fetish-gift the

Arumbayas give to Walker's expedition in *The Broken Ear*
brings catastrophe down on the anthropologists: used to hide
a gem protecting against poison (snakebite), it results in the
expedition being poisoned by curare, the deadly potion with
which the tribe anoint their blow-darts. When Mitsuhirato
learns that a messenger has set out to warn Tintin of his activities in *The Blue Lotus*, he gives him what Wang-Chen-yee
describes in the original French as a 'present' of Raijajah
juice, the poison of madness. Also lost in the English translation is Rastapopoulos's description of the dynamite with
which he intends to blow up the separatist guerrillas whose
help he has enlisted in *Flight 714*: *le plastic que je réservais
comme cadeau aux Sondonésiens* – 'the Semtex I was saving as
a present for the Sondonesians'. 'A present! Something spe-
cially for me, brought from his country, I expect. Dear little
fellow!' muses Haddock fondly as Abdullah runs off to fetch
him his gift in *The Red Sea Sharks*: a cuckoo-clock, a gift of
time. 'Why, it's magnificent, Abdullah!' Haddock purrs as he
holds it to his face. 'You see . . . to wind it up . . . you do that!'
snarls Abdullah, pulling the chain to make the bird jump out
and douse Haddock with water.

These gifts are all poisoned, booby-trapped. But the worst
gift of all is the gift of Louis XIV to Sir Francis: Marlinspike is
truly spiked. Why? Because, in substituting itself for acknow-
ledgement on Louis's part that his beloved Francis is his son,
it withholds the latter's *real* name, his identity, family relations, status and power. What recourse has Sir Francis, other
than to heap imaginative invective on the world in general?
Only one: to take some small form of revenge through his

own act of withholding. In the seventeenth century, naval officers of warring European nations were not only allowed but also positively encouraged to plunder enemy ships. They were, like Red Rackham, pirates – but 'licensed', 'legitimate' ones. But their piracy carried with it one non-negotiable condition: you had to give your plunder to the King. Sir Francis fails to do this. By extraordinary coincidence, it transpired after the publication of *The Secret of the Unicorn–Red Rackham's Treasure* that, unbeknown to Hergé, there had indeed been a naval captain named Haddock who was court-martialled in 1674 for not handing over profits he had made while on state business in Málaga – in other words, for tax evasion.

This is precisely Sir Francis's crime: tax evasion. He may get away with it, but its spectre will haunt his line for generations. 'Anything to declare, Captain?' asks Tintin as they pass through Syldavian customs in *Destination Moon*. 'Me? . . . Nothing at all!' replies Haddock; but when the customs officer finds endless whisky bottles hidden away in his suitcase, he begs to differ, fining him 875 Khors duty. Calculus is tuned into this one too: as he leaves Marlinspike at the end of *The Castafiore Emerald* he hears the word *emeraude* as *fraude* and tells the Captain: 'Certainly not . . . I never do . . . I make it a point of honour to declare everything at the customs,' a response that leaves Haddock shaking and biting his thumb in anger. If even the mistaken mention of the subject so rattles him, this is because it reminds him at some level of where his own money has come from. It is dishonourable, guilty money. Indeed, both sources of money are guilty: the King's official legacy to Sir Francis because it keeps a guilty secret of lost

127

honour, extra-marital defloration and subsequent non-recognition, and Sir Francis's illicit legacy (intended for his sons but received by his several-times-great-grandson) because it is secretly and illegally kept. Both sources of money are, like the de Lantys' fortune, bloodstained. And both sources take on a similar status when you learn that, while the French name for Louis XIV was the *Roi-Soleil* or Sun King, the less admiring Germans called him *Räuberkönig*, a Robber King, essentially no different from Red Rackham.

Just as the sculptor Balthazar withheld the fetish, hiding it in his trunk until his beneficiary found it without knowing what it was, Sir Francis withheld money. He withheld it from Louis XIV, the robber who stole his name and poisoned his life, leaving him and his descendants embittered. Sir Francis also stole it from Red Rackham, who stole it from the Spanish (as he boasts to Sir Francis, it is 'the booty we captured from a Spaniard' – in other words, a Spanish galleon – 'three days ago'), who stole it from the Incas. This money's 250-year passage and return makes Odysseus's twenty-year journey look like a short commute. What the four books from *The Secret of the Unicorn* through to *Prisoners of the Sun* do, essentially, is follow the money trail back to its source – or, rather, trails plural: that of the 'legitimate' (what a misnomer) and the illegitimate legacies of wealth. And both trails lead to the same place: the sun. One way or another, it is the sun's money: the Sun King's or Sun God's, a shard fallen from a star that keeps an almost infinite amount back in reserve. As the Inca tells Haddock, Tintin and Calculus when they marvel at the gold and diamonds with which their saddle bags have been stuffed,

'This is nothing compared with the riches of the temple . . . The treasure of the Incas, for which the Spanish conquerors searched in vain for so long.'

The sun: this is where Derrida starts his consideration of money in *Given Time*. 'The Sun and the King, the Sun-King will be the subjects of these lectures,' he tells us on the very first page. Later he compares Mauss's notion of 'returns' to 'the natural revolution of the Earth around the Sun, of the absolute sun at its high noon'. But the book begins by invoking the morning sun, via the figure of Madame de Maintenon, Louis XIV's mistress who, upon the Queen's death, became his morganatic wife – 'morganatic' meaning 'excluded from all noble titles and rights' and deriving from the low Latin *morganegiba*, 'gift of the morning'. De Maintenon was notoriously austere, and persuaded Louis to enforce laws with an iron first. That she should take so much trouble over the law and legitimacy seems paradoxical to Derrida, since she 'was also the governess of the royal bastards'. As a child, she experienced exile in Martinique, and her father was arrested as a forger. 'Everything in her life,' writes Derrida, 'seems to bear the most austere, the most rigorous, and the most authentic stamp of counterfeit money.'

Illegitimate children, illegitimate money: in the figure of de Maintenon, the two go hand in hand. Nor are they far apart in the *Tintin* books, where counterfeit money finds its way everywhere, penetrating even the law itself. Look at the opening sequence of *The Crab with the Golden Claws*: Thompson and Thomson call Tintin over to a café and buy him a drink. They have, they tell him proudly, been entrusted with 'a very important case': tracking counterfeit coins. 'Is it easy to spot one of these fakes?' asks Tintin. 'People like ourselves who have examined them can tell one in a flash, of course,' boasts one detective, tapping a coin to attract the waiter's attention and then paying him with it, 'but most people are easily fooled by them.' 'I'm sorry, Sir . . .' the waiter replies, dropping the coin disdainfully back onto the table: it is a dud. There is a deeper meaning lurking beneath this embarrassing episode: not only is Thompson and Thomson's money counterfeit, but they are also counterfeit themselves. As Léon and Alexis, they are illegitimate – and on top of that, fake aristocrats, common children dressed as little gentlemen, and on top of even that fake children of Remi. Hergé associates them with forgery time and again. In *The Black Island* (*The Forgers*) their photograph appears in the *Daily Reporter* directly beneath another of 'forged notes so perfect even bank cashiers are fooled'. Put on trial in *Tintin and the Picaros*, they are accused of 'duplicity' and immediately talk of their childhood, claiming to have 'been wearing moustaches since we were born'. No wonder they constantly get the time wrong: they, too, are awash in it, lost in the fraught economic cycles opened up by the bad gift. This is yet another meaning of their desert antics in *Land of Black Gold*: their departures and returns follow the path of time, big one-hour loops that lead them to find the petrol-can reserve they do not know that they themselves have lost as they trail after money (the reward on Tintin's head) under the hot noon, then one o'clock, then two o'clock sun.

How can you tell if money is 'good' or counterfeit? Mauss

claims that legitimate money in the strictest sense of the word emerges when precious things or signs of wealth are made into currency by being 'tested [*titrées*], depersonalised, detached from all relationships with any legal entity . . . other than the state that mints them'. Derrida picks up on the word *titrées* and finds that it comes from *titre*, 'title, qualification, fineness of alloyed gold or silver'. In order to earn its title as good money, money must be *titrée* or 'titrated', tested 'to ascertain', as the OED puts it, 'the amount of a constituent in the mixture' – and titrated by the state. 'Everything,' writes Derrida, 'turns around this value of title and the title of value.' Bad money is bad because it 'has no title'. This is Sir Francis Haddock's situation: Louis, the absolute head of state, withheld his true title and left him with a false name, 'Haddock' – a doubly poisoned gift. Why? Because in French 'haddock' is *aiglefin* or *aigrefin*, words which, besides denoting the fish, carry the figural connotation of *escroc* or 'swindler', 'fraudster', 'counterfeiter'. Triply poisoned: he is fake, his name is fake, and it means forger. And to top it all, Louis then confers upon him a title, not the one he should have, and for reasons that are, at best, disingenuous.

This is the legacy his descendant has inherited. Everything about the Captain bears the stamp of counterfeit. Look how he apes the forms of the aristocracy after coming into the château: the monocles, the pretentious diction ("Pon my word, it's Tintin!' he exclaims at the beginning of *The Seven Crystal Balls*, tucking his riding whip under his arm). Hergé could well have read the article in the March 1937 issue of *Le Crapouillot* entitled '*Noblesse d'Escroquerie*' or 'Fake

Nobility', describing frauds passing themselves off either as existing counts and countesses or inventing themselves as fictitious ones, in several cases taking names from novels (there was even one who called himself 'de Balzac'). Haddock oozes *noblesse d'escroquerie*. It is in his blood. He must sweat it, because even animals pick it up. His ancestor's title *le Chevalier* (a Knight or 'Sir' in English) literally means one who can ride a *cheval*, a horse. Haddock cannot. Horses throw him off their back at every opportunity, in the desert of *The Red Sea Sharks* as readily as in the fields outside his château in *The Seven Crystal Balls*. The only time he rides a horse successfully is in the factory in *Destination Moon*, and on that occasion the horse is fake, a pantomime one. Even horses' poor relations llamas can smell it, and spit contemptuously in his face.

Counterfeit, non-titration: Haddock, like Thompson and Thomson in *Tintin and the Picaros*, will be condemned to death for it, sacrificed on the altar of his own illegitimacy. This is the deeper truth of the Inca ritual in *Prisoners of the Sun*. As he boards the sea-plane and sets out towards the sun at the end of *The Seven Crystal Balls*, the first half of the two-book adventure, Nestor runs up to the quayside with a suitcase of spare monocles. The gag brilliantly sets up the climax of the second book, in which a giant monocle is used to light the pyre using the sun's own rays. Between the Sun King who gives money, time, life itself and now the gift of death and Haddock who receives it (on his 'birthday', his day of solar returns – and even this is fake) is the sign of his own fakeness, magnified and magnifying.

And yet both Haddock's and Thompson and Thomson's sacrifices are (of course) interrupted: Thompson and Thomson's by the arrival of a giant gold-crowned king-float with armed guerrillas in its mouth (we are, after all, in the middle of a revolution), Haddock's by the sun's own mini-revolution, its temporary departure and return. The Sun or King, or Sun King, reprieves them – that is, gives them time. And time comes rushing back: noon, two o'clock, the lot. *Il était moins cinq, n'est-ce pas?* Haddock asks one of the detectives as he unties him from the pole on which he has just faced the firing squad in *Tintin and the Picaros*: rendered into English as 'Saved by the bell, eh?' What the expression literally means is 'It was five minutes to, no?' *Je ne sais pas: ma montre est arrêtée*, the detective replies: 'I don't know: my watch has stopped.' The scientists whose information (the foreknowledge of the coming eclipse) saves Haddock after Tintin reads about it in the newspaper in *Prisoners of the Sun* are Swiss: watchmakers, measurers of time. Both Thompson and Thomson and Haddock are saved just in time, by time, for time.

But their rescues are not triumphant ones. The king who comes to the detectives' aid is fake, a gaudy carnival maquette who laughs over them grotesquely, disdaining even to look at them directly. Haddock's salvation is also a replay of his ancestral curse: the sun hides itself, refuses to appear, to gather him up into its heart. As soon as he is rejected ('saved') his foundations (the logs of the pyre) give way and he falls, ridiculous: released back into poisoned time, into inauthenticity.

ii

The expression 'looking for noon at two o'clock' comes from Baudelaire. To be precise, it comes from his single-page story of 1869 that lies at the heart of Derrida's book: *La Fausse Monnaie* or 'Counterfeit Money'.

The story goes as follows: the narrator and his friend walk out of a tobacconist's, pocketing their change. Just outside, they come across a beggar holding out his hat. Both put coins in it, but the friend's is bigger – worth quite a large amount, in fact. The narrator tells him: 'You are right; next to the pleasure of feeling surprise, there is none greater than to cause a surprise' – to which the friend replies: 'It was the counterfeit coin.' The narrator's brain, 'always concerned with looking for noon at two o'clock (what an exhausting faculty is nature's gift to me)', starts racing, reasoning that his friend's action was driven by 'the desire to create an event in this poor devil's life' and wondering what its consequence will be: will the counterfeit money multiply into real money in the beggar's hands, even make him wealthy? Or will it get him arrested? The narrator's fancy rages, 'lending wings to my friend's mind' – until the latter shatters his reverie by saying: 'Yes, you are right; there is no sweeter pleasure than to surprise a man by giving him more than he hopes for.' Upon hearing this, the narrator realises that his friend had simply been out 'to do a good deed while at the same time making a good deal; to earn forty cents and the heart of God; to win paradise economically; in short, to pick up gratis the certificate of a charitable man.' And this, he decides, sucks. To be mean is one thing, but to do evil out of stupidity is 'the most irreparable of vices'.

Derrida, as you might expect, picks up on lots of aspects of this story: the spectre of the law, the rhetoric of giving and lending ('nature's gift'; fancy 'lending wings') that surrounds the main event of a bad gift which itself forms part of a larger economic purchase (winning paradise economically) and so on. Most intriguingly, though, he homes in on the fact that the story begins as the two men leave a tobacconist's. This leads him on a long digression through the history of tobacco: its banning by Louis XIII, its use in primitive ritual, where it is linked to offering and sacrifice, and so on. From an economic point of view, Derrida notes, tobacco represents expenditure at pure loss: a luxury item, it goes up in smoke. But it also leaves remains, ashes, which maintain symbolic links to memory, death and inheritance. Baudelaire's story takes off from the change left over from the two friends' luxury expenditure: like the coin itself, it proceeds from the remainder.

Let's, on no more than a whim, embark on our own digression through tobacco in the *Tintin* books and see if we get any change from it. The obvious place to start would be *Cigars of the Pharaoh*, in which tobacco is in the title and all over: littering the mouth of the tomb and stuffed into the mouth of the law in the dream inside the tomb (Thompson and Thomson are shown smoking fat cigars), stashed in a safe in the colonel's office and stored in a courtesy cabinet in the Maharaja's palace. This tobacco's trail leads to the eponymous *fumerie* Tintin rumbles in the follow-up book, *The Blue Lotus*, a smoking-den where the opium hidden in the last book's cigars is consumed: the secret was wrapped in tobacco the whole time. When Tintin visits Balthazar's flat near the beginning of the next adventure, *The Broken Ear*, he learns that the sculptor always had a pipe in his mouth and, noticing a cigarette butt on the floor, realises that someone else must have been there too. As in the vault of Kih-Oskh, tobacco, or its remainder, betrays the presence of the stranger in the home (or tomb, which is what Balthazar's home has become, a point emphasised when Snowy contemplates a skull).

Tobacco seems to go hand in hand with the uneasy host–guest relationships dotted throughout the *Tintin* books. The uninvited 'foreign persons' who pitch their tents in Marlinspike's state rooms in *The Red Sea Sharks*, pushing Haddock's knight outfits into the background, smoke big hookahs. Haddock's realisation that he is effectively a prisoner in his swanky Los Dopicos hotel room in *Tintin and the Picaros* dawns when he is prevented from leaving to buy tobacco and then, the next morning, given a huge police escort to a small tobacconist's. In that book, the king who saves Thompson and Thomson holds a giant cigar in his hand; the charmless Peggy, meanwhile, who has already nagged her husband Alcazar about the number of cigars he smokes, tells him to stop dropping ashes all over the palace that he has promised – and delivered to – her. Let's not forget that Castafiore, whose arrival interrupted Haddock's pipe-stuffing two books previously, stayed in Marlinspike's Louis XIII bedroom.

Tobacco in Hergé's work, then, opens into questions of the law, of hospitality and legacy. But most interestingly, it also accompanies fakeness. The cigars of the Pharaoh are fake ones. In *King Ottokar's Sceptre* Tintin begins to suspect that the chain-smoking Alembick, who constantly drops butts on the floor, may be an impostor when the sigillographer shuns the cigarettes on offer at a mobile kiosk in Prague Airport. He is an impostor – and when the switch takes place and Tintin hears the real Alembick's screams over the phone, he rushes out past a big poster advertising the (Ancient Egyptian-themed) ISIS Cigarettes. Another cigarette brand appears in the detectives' drawer whose contents Tintin inspects in the following book, *The Crab with the Golden Claws*: next to five counterfeit coins and a strip of paper bearing the almost-erased name *Karaboudjan* (the first three letters of which Tintin will slowly spell out as he scrutinises them through a magnifying glass – 'There's "K" . . . and an "A" . . . and that's an "R" . . .' – thus naming the Syldavian for 'King'), lies a pack of ARISTOS cigarettes. The arrangement of these objects is absolutely stuffed with significance: from it, the whole story of the fakeness embodied by Thompson and Thomson (and by the *Karaboudjan*'s captain, Haddock) stares us right in the face. But the full scope of what tobacco reveals (or conceals) can be made out through the smokescreen of two longer sequences.

The first begins in the pursuit of tobacco, in *The Calculus Affair*. This book, like *Cigars of the Pharaoh*, is one long tobacco-trail. Tintin and Haddock smell tobacco in the non-smoking Professor's laboratory, surprise an intruder from whose pocket falls a pack of cigarettes bearing the name of the hotel Calculus is booked into in Geneva and, setting out to protect their friend, find the same brand in Professor Topolino's house in Nyon, then again when a lit fag-end is thrown at them from a diplomatic car. But the sequence we are interested in starts, like Baudelaire's story, at the entrance to a tobacconist's. Haddock, noticing the tobacco sign that hangs beside a knight's shield on the shop's front (he and Tintin have wandered past a statue of a knight the previous day), crosses the road to buy a refill for his pipe. While doing this, he is hit by a car. He turns out to be unhurt, and Tintin persuades the car's Italian driver to take them in pursuit of the Chrysler containing the kidnapped Calculus.

As they drive, Tintin tells the Italian the whole story of the kidnapping, the secret ultrasonic weapon, the competing secret services and so on. The Italian drives recklessly and, after causing havoc by speeding through a village on market day, is stopped by a gendarme who, preparing to throw the book at him, demands his name. This turns out to be so long and aristocratic (Arturo Benedetto Giovanni Giuseppe Pietro Archangelo Alfredo Cartoffoli da Milano) that the cop, daunted by the task of writing it down, simply replies: 'Er . . . I . . . Hm . . . Well, don't do it again . . .' Speeding off again, they soon catch up with the Chrysler and, not finding Calculus in it, order its occupants to open the boot. They comply, but it is empty: Calculus, as it turns out later, is hidden in a secret compartment under the back seat. The Chrysler leaves, and Arturo Benedetto da Milano angrily accuses them of making the whole story up to cadge a lift off him before speeding off again. Abandoned at the roadside, the Captain lights a pipe, burning himself on the match.

So much is at play here. Besides the law, and the aristocratic name which places one above the law, there is the whole issue of *credit* or credence, and its flip side, accounting and accountability. Tintin and Haddock present a story to Arturo, an account that Arturo ends up failing to believe. This rejection repeats the rejection of the previous night, during which Haddock made an SOS call from a helicopter which was picked up by radio ham Jolyon Wagg, who steadfastly refused to credit Haddock's account of himself and his situation, roaring with laughter: 'You old humbug, you! . . . Get away, Haddock!' Two days later the Bordurian police in the Fortress of Bakhine will believe his story, but they should not: his stammering and sweating alone should alert them to the fact that he is fake, in disguise, merely passing as a member of the Red Cross. This book, which begins with the disintegration of Haddock's reflection in a mirror, perfectly counterbalances the anguish of not being credited for being what you are with the guilt that comes from pretending to be what you are not. And it does so alongside a series of attempts, always frustrated, for Haddock to smoke his pipe in peace. On the book's final page his last attempt to light it makes him burn himself on the microfilmed plans which Calculus holds out above his match – that is, on the secret itself.

But there is more: the car-chase sequence is suffused with an anxiety about time. As Arturo speeds away from the policeman, he grits his teeth and says: 'Now we make up for the lost time . . . Avanti!' After opening his boot, the indignant owner of the Chrysler shouts: 'You've wasted enough of my time already!' This anxiety runs through the whole book: they keep being just too late to rescue Calculus, missing him at the hotel, missing the train on which he leaves Geneva. The book's dialogue is full of time: 'All to gain time . . .', 'If you hurry you'll still catch him,' 'Let's hope we'll be in time,' 'You're too late, sir,' 'Let's hope we can get there before it's too late,' 'Let's hope we're not too late . . .' Haddock and Tintin are constantly lagging behind, looking for noon at two o'clock, running after the sun. In this respect, 'Calculus's real name is vital. In the original French it is *Tournesol*, 'Sunflower', literally 'turn-sun' due to sunflowers' (or, to give them their more scientific name, 'heliotropes') propensity to turn throughout the day as they follow the sun's path. What Tintin and Haddock fail to find due to the Chrysler's double-chamber ('I'll be generous,' says the owner, showing them the boot in order to withhold what they are really looking for) is, if not the sun itself, then the one who turns towards the sun, whose very name turns through its high noon. The heliotropic aspect of Calculus-Tournesol's name is much, much more than just a chance of naming, as we shall soon see.

The second sequence is one in whose middle comes an act of prohibition of tobacco. This sequence, from *Flight 714*, contains a scene that has so many points of correspondence with Baudelaire's story that, again, it is hard to believe Hergé did not have it floating around in the back of his mind. Hergé's setting is Jakarta Airport, that is, the tropics, where the sun never deviates much from its high noon – a point that Haddock makes to himself when he sees a poor man sneezing so hard that his hat comes off: 'one of life's failures . . . even catches cold in the tropics', he thinks. Handing the man's hat back he, like Baudelaire's narrator's friend, slips money into it: a five-dollar bill. Then, like the narrator, he begins speculating about what the poor man will do when, to his great surprise, he finds this large amount of money. 'What's this? . . . Am I dreaming? It can't be . . . a five dollar bill!' he imagines the poor man gasping. 'Heaven be praised! At last I can buy food!' Tears spill from Haddock's eyes as he sees him in his mind chomping on sandwiches and asking God between burps to 'bless the noble and generous soul who has taken pity on my misery'. 'My good deed for the day,' he tells himself.

Haddock acts from a motivation to do both what Baudelaire's narrator first credits his friend with attempting *and* what he eventually realises the friend actually wants: he has, as far as he is concerned, provoked an event *and* earned the heart of God: won paradise relatively economically. Not gratis: his five-dollar bill is real. There is nothing wrong with his money. The problem is with the poor man: he is not a poor man. He turns out a few minutes later to be a multi-millionaire: Laszlo Carreidas, of Carreidas aircraft, cloth, oil, stores, newspapers and Sani-Cola. When Haddock and his entourage are introduced to him, we have (not for the first time in the books) an act of prestidigitation as Calculus, with a 'Presto!', plucks the five-dollar bill from Carreidas's hat. 'You're a trespi . . . no, I mean . . . presti . . . prestigidi . . . prestidigita . . . ta . . . ta . . . TAAAH . . . AAAH . . . HA HA HA HA HA HA . . . prestidigitator!' roars Carreidas, collapsing between sneezes and laughter: to his mind, Calculus has just performed the conjuror's trick of pulling money out of nowhere, from thin air. In this seemingly trivial episode, the spotlight is turned once more on the provenance of money. That, and its destination, will develop into the book's main drivers.

Carreidas asks Haddock if he likes Battleships. 'One of my ancestors went in for that sort of thing,' Haddock replies. Carreidas means the game, though: he likes playing it in his private jet. He invites Haddock, Tintin and Calculus to join him on it (they are flying to the same International Astronautical Congress in Sydney). They decline, but he insists. Installed on his plane as a less-than-willing guest, Haddock takes out his pipe, but Carreidas tells him: 'Smoking is strictly prohibited, Captain. Even the smell of tobacco upsets me.' Haddock pockets his pipe again, and they play Battleships. Carreidas cheats, using a CCTV camera to spy on the Captain's table. Tintin begins to suspect that all is not right on this plane, and has his worries confirmed when it is hijacked by Carreidas's own staff, who, descending to below-radar altitude, divert it to the island on which Rastapopoulos awaits. When Rastapopoulos explains that he wants Carreidas's money, which is stashed away in a Swiss bank under a false name, we are plunged once more into a drama of tax evasion and counterfeit identity.

Carreidas is falsely poor and dubiously rich. Rastapopoulos has learnt to forge his false signature; all he needs is the account number. He has Carreidas injected with a truth serum that he hopes will make him divulge this, but instead the millionaire starts confessing all his fraudulent, deceptive acts since childhood. Flailing in fury at the doctor who administered the serum, Rastapopoulos pricks himself with the syringe, and starts confessing his own duplicity, claiming to be worse than Carreidas while the latter scoffs back, 'Peanuts! Kid's stuff!' and gives more examples of his own deceptiveness. Thus the tug of war between the two men for a bank account becomes a battle of accounts, of self-account-ancy: each man backs up his argument with a precise, itemised list of his misdemeanours – whom he has swindled or intends to swindle, when, how, and how much.

But as the two men blur together arguing who is more evil, their exchanges and equivalences are themselves a piece of prestidigitation: we should always look the other way, look two links down the chain. 'One of my ancestors went in for that sort of thing.' Who is the real cheater at the game of Battleships? Whose money came from tax evasion long before either of these two were conceived? Whose very name means 'swindler'? Another meaning of *escroc* is 'one who cheats at games'. This whole adventure, which began with Haddock's gift of five dollars to Carreidas and his distracted bumping into Skut while he contemplated it afterwards, looking for noon at two o'clock, acts out his own ancestral curse. Through his giving, he has yet again replayed his trauma, caused it to re-enact itself (albeit, of course, in disguise) in front of him. The poor man whose millions will not bring him any closer to the sun is, ultimately, none other than himself.

In this book, Carreidas (notice, again, the KAR ('King') lurking in his name) plays the role of Louis XIII. 'No one smokes in the presence of Laszlo Carreidas!' he booms, even as he is tied up. Rastapopoulos responds by blowing cigar smoke in his face. Smoke will be everywhere by the book's end: poisonous, sulphurous smoke brewed up in a volcano. 'And what about all this smoke?' complains Carreidas. 'Me with my sensitive throat! Are you trying to kill me?' The volcano eventually erupts, blowing into the sky a column of smoke more than thirty thousand feet high. Haddock and his entourage are saved by an observation plane, but found to be suffering from collective amnesia about the whole adventure. Their memories of it have been absolutely wiped, erased; they have undergone, to borrow a term we met earlier, 'radical forgetting'. It took alien intervention to bring it about, but nonetheless they have become recipients of Derrida's impossible, *genuine* gift – the gift that does not impose terms as it opens up time around obligation and indebtedness but instead wipes the slate clean, smashes the slate itself. In a way, *Flight 714* is the most positive of all the *Tintin* books because it moves from a bad gift to a *real* gift which takes bad, noxious time away, sends it up in smoke, expends it at pure loss.

The only remnant from it is a piece of metal. After Calculus finds in his pocket a hemispherically-headed rod which sends his pendulum spinning in frantic revolutions, he has it analysed – tested, titrated – in the laboratories at Jakarta University. It turns out to be 'composed of cobalt in the natural state, alloyed with iron and nickel', something unknown, not found on this earth, under this sun. The change from all that smoke is – for once – a pure, a unique coin.

For Derrida, Baudelaire's *La Fausse Monnaie* or

'Counterfeit Money' is allegorical. What it represents is nothing less than the birth of literature. Why? Because it shows an
'event', a 'history' created by a simulacrum, by fake currency,
in conjunction with an 'I' who is aligned with nature (the
recipient of its 'gift') but in fact is merely passing off as natural: as a character in a story, the narrator is also a simulacrum,
as fictive as the coin. Like him, says Derrida, literature 'can
only consist in passing itself off as natural' – and in constitut-
ing nature itself through a set of monetary processes:
exchange, credit, bequeathing, lending, giving. Not only *is* literature counterfeit, *through* literature, the 'natural' can be
seen to be counterfeit as well, a construct passing itself off as
an absolute truth. The real truth, though, is the paradox that
for both literature and nature, the counterfeit is the pre-condition of the 'real': the very *notions* of the 'real' and 'natural'
are generated and sustained through an elaborate economy of
cultural conventions – artificial signs that, having done their
job, pretend merely to represent the very thing they have
created.

But Derrida has one more question: is the friend's coin
really counterfeit after all? He tells the narrator it is, but how
do we know he is not just playing with him, 'creating an event'
in his life? It is a good question, and one we should also ask.
Our version of it would be: how do we know that Sir Francis
is actually the son of Louis XIV? Can we DNA-test or titrate
him? No. Ultimately, our answer is the same one Derrida
receives: we do not know; we cannot know; and beyond us
Baudelaire does not and cannot know, and Hergé does not
and cannot know. Even if they have an opinion on the matter,

it is beyond their control as much as ours to determine the answer definitively, given the possibilities active within or activated by their work. Here we come across another, fundamental piece of withholding: kept in reserve by any text, says Derrida, is a secret 'eternally unreadable, absolutely indecipherable, even refusing itself to any promise of deciphering or hermeneutic'. The text creates the secret, and the secret underpins the text, making it readable through its own unreadability. It is 'a secret whose possibility assures the possibility of literature'. And in literature, the secret remains 'infinitely private because public through and through', stays hidden even as it is spread on the surface of the page, as obvious as a bank note, a letter of credit or a silver two-franc piece – or, he might have added, three overlaid parchments.

Derrida ends *Given Time* with a final turn towards the sun, by invoking the figure of Icarus. In his earlier 1971 essay 'White Mythology: Metaphor in the Text of Philosophy' this turning towards the sun is done by heliotropes, sunflowers. Here, it is the birth of philosophy that is under the microscope. The 'natural truth' of philosophy, writes Derrida, is constructed through the exchange of fictive, poetic mechanisms, metaphors which erase themselves as metaphors, like coins whose symbols have been rubbed away. In other words, the secret of philosophy is literature. The title 'White Mythology' refers to the writer Anatole France's 1894 novel *The Garden of Epicurus*, whose protagonist Polyphilos describes philosophy as 'anaemic mythology' – anaemic because it has been drained of colour in order to acquire its status as 'truth'.

How, then, can philosophy deal with the question of metaphor itself? 'Only around a blind spot or central deafness,' writes Derrida. Looking at philosophers' attempts to do this, he is drawn to the example of metaphor that Aristotle favours in his *Poetics*: the sun casting forth light like a sower casting forth seeds. Wait a minute, Derrida says: when was it ever *seen* that the sun 'casts forth' light? The analogy relies on 'a long and hardly visible chain' of associations held together within language. But Aristotle's choice of the sun is a good one, he continues, because all metaphors are heliotropic: they turn towards what is supposedly absolutely present and visible, and what is more absolutely present and visible than the sun? Is not the sun the very pre-condition of all presence and all visibility? And yet the sun is never wholly present within language; how could it be? It, too, turns, via all the figures, or 'tropes', of light and vision that pervade philosophy's rhetoric of knowledge and understanding (clarity, insight, perception, illumination – they are everywhere). Metaphor, then, is doubly heliotropic: it is both the movement of sunflowers as they turn after the sun on the horizon *and* the turning of the (always metaphorical) sun itself within language. And notions of the true, the natural, are born of metaphor's double-twist, its solar-floral prestidigitation – plucked from its hat, as it were. While classical philosophy turns always to the 'true', absolute sun, Derrida proposes that a more adventurous, poetic version of philosophy should let the absolute itself be taken captive, held to ransom, even disgorged at every moment in the twists and turns of language. To put it metaphorically: poetic and adventurous philosophy should collapse the sun into a sunflower and unfold it without limit, rupturing the horizon's line, wresting open its circle.

Where is this new detour through secrets and sunflowers leading us? To the west, via Calculus – or, to restore to him his proper name, Tournesol: the turning flower who turns people into flowers via their names and people from their habits via flowers. As Abdullah finds out when he pushes him, *Tournesol tourne*: Tournesol turns, and turns, and turns. If he constantly mishears things, this is because the Epicurean Garden in which his flowerbed lies is located extremely close to the spot of central deafness that Derrida describes. Always twisting and mutating meanings, he is a principle of tropism, a tropic agent. On his entry to the books, he copies nature to make a submarine, giving his friends access to the bed of history. Returning from there, he makes money on the basis of his simulacrum. It is this money that returns Haddock to his home, completing his Odyssean circle, as we have seen. Later, as we have also seen, drawn westwards again by the sun, he distrusts the veracity of what the sun illuminates as it approaches its high noon, perceiving it as metaphor, which in fact it is. He, just as much as the others, is held by the force-field of the secret – but he takes a different route through this, sliding sideways, turning words around, detouring through flowers, names, minerals to meaning. Tournesol is metaphor in action. While Tintin and Haddock track the secret and believe – mistakenly – that they have found it, he concerns himself with tropism's embodiment, the pendulum, whose unending movement, rather than confirming the certainty of truth, unfolds it without limit. Philosophically and poetically speaking, Calculus the scientist is the real hero of the *Tintin* books.

Before we leave the sun, one final turn. In both Derrida's texts that we have looked at, the remarkable novelist, anthropologist and philosopher Georges Bataille (the author of *Literature and Evil* whom we briefly met earlier) pops up. His work is cited as a shining example of the adventurous, poetic thinking advocated at the end of 'White Mythology'. It is full to bursting with the sun: from sunlight splashing down on cobblestones in the 1957 novel *Blue of Noon* 'as though light could splinter and kill' to the notions of limitless solar generosity, expenditure without return, expounded in the 1949 study *The Accursed Share*. Most interesting to us here, though, is the short 1930 essay 'Sacrificial Mutilation and the Severed Ear of Van Gogh'. Bataille is drawn to Van Gogh by what he calls the painter's 'solar obsession', the 'overwhelming relations he maintained with the sun' – as evidenced, for example, in the 'Sower' paintings he did at Arles in 1888, which show sunsets so vivid they are virtually unbearable, or his 'Sunflower' series, whose subjects seem to writhe and threaten to take over all of space. These lead Bataille to suspect that the truth of Van Gogh's auto-mutilation (cutting off his ear), and the truth of sacrifice in general, lies in imitating, winning heaven and being infinitely generous. Why? Because both are driven by a desire 'to resemble perfectly an ideal term, generally described in mythology as a solar god who rips and tears out his own organs'.

iii

Which brings us back to *The Broken Ear*. Balthazar, the sculptor who makes a resemblance of the fetish with the eponymous mutilated organ, has received some acclaim from critics for his primitivist style. In him, the logic of the primitive meets the logic of art. The *use* to which he puts his art is copying, imitating, making resemble. That is what he does with the fetish and that is what his art does in general. 'Just look at those flowers,' his landlady says to Tintin as she stares at the Van Gogh-like painting in his attic; 'you can almost smell them' – in French, *Comme elles sont naturelles; on dirait qu'elles vont rire*: 'How natural they are; you'd say they were about to laugh.'

The landlady is touching on a very classical motif here: mimesis. Derived from the mimosa flower, whose contortions when you touch it mimic the grimaces of a mime, 'mimesis' is the principle that art should imitate nature, copy what is real. Established by Aristotle, the concept was reprised in the Renaissance, where it became very important among artists and writers, many of whom believed that their task was, as Shakespeare's Hamlet puts it, simply to 'hold, as t'were, the mirror up to nature'. Shakespeare chews the concept over throughout his work, and nowhere more so than in *The Sonnets*, where a fascinating set of twists and turns balances questions of beauty, creation, 'fathering' or 'generating' something or someone, inheritance, identity and resemblance around the fraught issue of the copy. The sequence of 154 poems is primarily addressed to an anonymous young man who has grown over time to be beautiful. But against that inevitable moment when, as he puts it in *Sonnet 60*, 'Time that gave, doth now his gift confound', Shakespeare urges him to reproduce:

> O that you were yourself, but love you are
> No longer yours, than you yourself here live,
> Against this coming end you should prepare,
> And your sweet semblance to some other give.
> So should that beauty which you hold in lease
> Find no determination, then you were
> Your self again after your self's decease,
> When your sweet issue your sweet form should bear.

Here, in *Sonnet 13*, Shakespeare is telling his young friend (with whom he is clearly in love himself) to breed, but he is using a barrage of economic metaphors to say this: giving, lease and issue – not to mention metaphors of 'semblance' and 'form'. Two sonnets before this, he uses an artisanal metaphor: nature, he tells the young man in *Sonnet 11*,

> carved thee for her seal, and meant thereby
> Thou shouldst print more, not let that copy die.

In other words, having a child is like printing a copy of a seal carved by an artisan. Another artisanal metaphor crops up in *Sonnet 15*:

All in war with Time for love of you,
As he takes from you, I engraft you new.

Grafting, as Calculus would know, is a botanical process whereby a shoot from one plant (often a dying one) is placed into a slit within another so that it can either continue growing itself or be reproduced by the host plant, depending on which way you look at it. But here Shakespeare is applying it to his own art, that is, to the process of writing: in writing about you, he is saying, I can reproduce your beauty, which will continue flourishing within my poem even as it fades in you. My artifice is as good as nature. Three sonnets later he repeats the claim: there is no point likening the fresh, beautiful young man to a summer's day because a summer's day, and summer itself, fades;

But thy eternal summer shall not fade,
Nor lose possession of that fair thou ow'st,
Nor shall death brag thou wandrest in his shade,
When in eternal lines to time thou grow'st.

The 'eternal lines' are the lines of the poem, which will continue reproducing the young man forever:

So long as men can breathe or eyes can see,
So long lives this, and this gives life to thee.

My artifice is *better than* nature, he is saying now. But as the sonnet sequence progresses further it becomes more complicated. Shakespeare claims in *Sonnet 53* not only that his writing copies the young man's beauty to perfection, but also that the young man *himself* copies culture and art, simply by existing in his natural state:

> Describe Adonis and the counterfeit
> Is poorly imitated after you,
> On Helen's cheek all art of beauty set
> And you in Grecian tires are painted new . . .

You are better than a description or resemblance of Adonis; if there is a 'counterfeit', it will have been imitated not after Adonis but after you. In other words, you will become the original, ousting the god himself; and the same thing goes for a painting of Helen of Troy (it is interesting that Shakespeare has his friend combine both male and female prototypes). Fifteen sonnets later, he renounces all artifice and skill in favour of the nature 'stored' up (an economic metaphor, of course) in the man's face, the very nature Shakespeare previously rejected as inferior to his art:

> And him as for a map doth Nature store,
> To show false Art what beauty was of yore.

The battle between nature and artifice is unresolved, it seems, oscillating in favour of first one and then the other. What is constant, though, is the mechanism or currency of *copying*: that is the criteria, the practice, the yardstick through which the value of either side might be measured. Whichever one can make a copy so good that it *lives* and assumes the mantle of the 'original' will be the better one. It is all about skill and craft – and its opposite, faulty craft, bad artisanship: 'false Art', 'poorly imitated'.

Which brings us back, again, to Balthazar: he imitates the fetish poorly. The critics may like him, but in the work he does for Tortilla he shows himself to be a shoddy craftsman, a bad counterfeiter. This, though, is not the real issue (even the Museum of Ethnography's curator does not notice the lapse). What *really* throws a spanner in the work of imitation and substitution is that he makes *two* copies. Here is another ultra-classical motif (in fact, the whole of Greek aesthetics is played out one way or another in Balthazar's attic), a motif that is both tied inextricably to mimesis and also mimesis's worst enemy: the simulacrum. This concept is Plato's. For him, everything is a copy: trees, chairs, tables, you and me – all material copies from divine and pure originals. That is all fine – but Plato gets very worked up in *The Sophist* by the notion of the 'simulacrum', because it is a copy without an original, an extra factor that screws up the whole symmetry of correspondence between copy and original. This is what Balthazar has done: thrown a simulacrum-spanner into the machinery and screwed it up. From almost the outset of *The Broken Ear*, there is one copy too many.

This is the problem within *Sarrasine* as well. As we have seen, the whole novella turns around copying, replication. La Zambinella is copied as a statue which is copied as Adonis which is copied as Endymion. Whether they are well copied or badly copied is not vital for the story: what is vital, and proves catastrophic for Sarrasine, is that he copies what was *already* a copy. La Zambinella, the original for Vien's 'counterfeit' Adonis and, of course, for Sarrasine's sculpture, is herself a counterfeit, an artificial woman posing as a natural one. Through her, a simulacrum jams the machinery of mimesis right from the very outset. Sarrasine sees in her face and body the wonders Greek chisels laboured to imitate without realising that it is precisely due to chisels and paint – not to mention knives – labouring to copy and combine classical conventions that 'her' face and body are the way they are in the first place.

For Barthes, this one copy too many leads us to the heart of realism just as much as the fullness/emptiness question did: in a vital respect, what we are seeing in *Sarrasine* is realism itself coming to grief around the very issue – copying – on which it sets its store. The real drama of the novella is the discovery that realism is 'badly named' since actually it 'consists not in copying the real but in copying a (depicted) copy of the real'. A copy of a copy even: Barthes writes that 'the "realistic" artist never places reality at the origin of his discourse, but only and always, as far back as can be traced, an already written real, a prospective code, along which we discern, as far as the eye can see, only a succession of copies'. Simulacra, lodged in the mimosa flowers like artificial worms, right back to the first ungrafted generation. The revelation of this fact brings about what Barthes, using the same type of economic metaphor as Derrida and Shakespeare, calls 'a generalised collapse of all economies: the economy of language . . . the economy of genders . . . the economy of the body . . . the economy of money'.

With this collapse, 'it is no longer possible to safeguard an order of equivalence; in a word it is no longer possible to represent'.

What is *The Broken Ear* really about? What lies at its core? A diamond? Or a chain of replications? The revelation of the diamond's existence comes almost casually, halfway through the book. Much more dramatic are Tintin's initial discovery that the fetish returned to the museum is a counterfeit and the final, climactic discovery (in Balthazar's brother's workshop, where Tintin sees scores of copied fetishes being hammered out and packaged into boxes) of mass-replication. This second discovery makes him jump up in the air with shock. Here, as with *Sarrasine*, mass-replication causes a virtual economic collapse: from £100 for one fetish to £17.50 for two to who-knows-how-little for who-knows-how-many. The diamond, as we have seen, slips away, but the copies are still out there, generating more copies, just as Sarrasine's copy of la Zambinella keeps on getting copied after his demise. If the fetish is even more mutilated at the book's end than it was at its beginning, this is perhaps because it has itself been sacrificed – literally disgorged, had 'its own organs ripped and torn out', to borrow Bataille's phrase – on the altar not of greed but of resemblance, of mimesis and its destructive underbelly, the simulacrum.

The culture of the copy: this is what Tintin confronts in *The Broken Ear,* and it is what he sees emerging in America even earlier: mass-replication that collapses the difference between tins, cars and knights, between cows, cats, dogs and people – and all against the Great Depression's background of general economic collapse. It is what he encounters in the Castle of Ben Mor: mass-replication of imitation money that threatens economy itself. For Plato, the issue of the simulacrum lies at the heart of the question of 'Art', and makes it a deeply problematic category. In a sense, this is what Hergé's work was always about too. This is the anxiety working its way to the surface in his many revisitings of the theme of simulacra, detouring through other contexts until it emerges properly. If the forgers of *The Black Island* have works of avant-garde art in their HQ and Carreidas takes time off in the middle of *Flight 714*'s cryptic replays of fraudulence and illegitimacy in order to buy art over the phone ('Three Picassos, two Bracques and a Renoir . . . Junk!' he snorts, then, hearing that Onassis is after them too, barks: 'Get them all! . . . I don't care how much, buy!'), by the final work, all detours have been cut out, and the problem of art unfolds on centre stage.

Tintin and Alph-Art, published in rough draft form in 1986, three years after Hergé's death, is based on the Fernand Legros scandal. Legros, a flamboyant international art dealer with a magnetic personality, was convicted in 1978 of selling fake works of modernist art – so many that to this day it is widely suspected that a considerable proportion of the Matisses, Modiglianis and Dufys that adorn the walls of private collections and public museums are in fact forgeries. He did not forge the work himself: like Tortilla, he got a minor artist to do it for him, one Elmyr de Hory. To sell a major work of art you need a 'provenance certificate' which proves that the work is genuine and has come legitimately onto the market; Legros would bribe and bully fellow dealers into issuing these. In

157

Hergé's version of the story, Legros becomes the charismatic guru Endaddine Akass, who has two art dealers bumped off when they refuse to sign provenance certificates for him (the least plausible episode of the entire *oeuvre*: as anyone actually involved with the art world would know, speaking with elephants and being memory-wiped by aliens is more credible than finding two honest art dealers in the same town). Their disappearance, which goes hand in hand with the rise of the avant-garde movement known as Alph-Art, in which giant letters are presented as artworks in and of themselves, raises Tintin's suspicions, drawing him into what will be his last adventure.

Some of the early scenes of *Tintin and Alph-Art* take the form almost of Platonic dialogues, dramatised theoretical discussions about art itself. One of their participants, Castafiore, paraphrases Georges Bataille's 1955 essay 'Lascaux or the Birth of Art', referencing the cave paintings of Lascaux and talking about the origins of civilisation. Haddock repeatedly argues that 'art has no use'. After passing these conceptual appetisers around for a while, Hergé starts uncovering and serving up the deeper and more essential Platonic truth of art: that it is fake, that its whole currency is fakeness. What Tintin eventually discovers is that the language and practice of Alph-Art – that is, of the avant-garde – is a cover for a giant forgery operation. Sneaking out of his bedroom in Akass's luxury house (in which, once more, he is a nominal guest and actual prisoner), he comes across a room full of paintings: 'A Modigliani! It's still wet! . . . And here's a Léger . . . a Renoir . . . a Picasso . . . A Gauguin . . . A Manet . . . A veritable factory of faking pictures, and perfect imitations, too!' Balthazar's brother's work-shop has come round again, but in a much more sinister form. Tintin, on discovering it, is led off to be killed, just as Sarrasine was after he stumbled across the fakeness at the core of art.

Sarrasine makes a copy and hopes that this will lead him to the real. He wants the real and the copy to merge. But what the copy brings him to is death. Balthazar's copying brings him death too. Perhaps Serres is wide of the mark: it is not the fetish that kills but the copying, the chain of replications itself. For Shakespeare, copying could reproduce life. Not for Balzac: 'You who can give life to nothing,' Sarrasine shouts at la Zambinella. Despite what Balthazar's landlady says, it would seem that Hergé is with Balzac and not Shakespeare on this one. Copies may breed copies, but they do not breed nature. Hergé, himself infertile, used natural, paternal language when discussing Tintin: 'I brought him up, protected him, nourished him, like a father brings up his child,' he tells Sadoul. To his first wife, Germaine, he wrote that Tintin 'wanted to become human' – that is, *he* wanted Tintin to become human. Like Sarrasine, he wanted the real behind the simulacrum – and we know by now where that leads. The final sequence of *Tintin and Alph-Art* – and of the whole *oeuvre* – reads like a snuff movie: not of Tintin, ultimately, but of Hergé. Tintin is to be killed by having liquid polyester poured over him and thus being turned into an 'expanded' sculpture entitled 'Reporter' ('You should be glad, your corpse will be displayed in a museum,' Akass tells him mockingly). The original reporter will be inserted into the reporter simulacrum.

The copy and the real will merge. And at the moment this takes place, Hergé will die.

Adonis and his counterfeit, giving death. This is the *moira* of Hergé's own white mythology, his anaemic destiny: to become Sarrasine to Tintin's la Zambinella. Realising this should prompt us to look back over the *Tintin* books and do yet one more corrective shift, a shift to a perspective point from which the hero himself takes on a sinister air. What if the equivalences and exchanges between Rastapopoulos, Carreidas *and* Haddock were themselves an elaborate piece of prestidigitation, and the real villain was hiding one more link down the chain? What if Castafiore were a feint, a stand-in for a castration already active from the work's beginning? Who is *really* androgynous? Who, like Faust, looks young at fifty? Tintin was duplicating himself as early as America, where he left a dummy-Tintin in a hotel window. What if even the 'original' Arumbaya fetish were a copy, a repetition (and not the last) of a deadly sculpture we have already met but had forgotten? Tintin was carved in wood and worshipped as a totem in the Congo. Even in Russia he became a 'statue', frozen in a block of ice. Might not the icy, white expanses of Hergé's nightmares really have their analogue in his own hero? Sadoul sees in the snows of Tibet a terror that comes from 'too much purity, too much innocence', and in the dreams 'an opening up to the Infinite, the Infinite which is the void' – that is, a huge space full of nothing.

Everybody wants to be Tintin: generation after generation. In a world of Rastapopouloses, Tricklers and Carreidases – or, more prosaically, Jolyon Waggs and Bolt-the-builders – Tintin represents an unattainable ideal of goodness, cleanness, authenticity. Apostolidès, pondering *The Broken Ear*, claims that Tintin is like the fetish as, despite being surrounded by corruption, he has a pure soul. Apostolidès is so close and yet so wrong: Tintin is like the fetish alright – but this is because, like Conrad's Kurtz, he is 'hollow at the core'. 'An empty hero', Tisseron calls him, 'void of all identity'; 'a blank domino', writes Serres, 'the empty and transparent circle'. The 'degree zero of typeage', he is also the degree zero of character, of history, of life itself. Beautiful, seductive, he is, like Balzac's castrato, the vanishing point of all desire. The black dots of his eyes are the opposite of every sun, his skin the antitype of any colour. Tintin is pure negative, the whiteness of the whale, the sexlessness of the unconsummated marriage, the radical erasure of the Khamsin. In *The Blue Lotus* Dawson complains that he and his network of accomplices are *toujours tenus en échec par ce gamin!* – 'always frustrated by this kid!'. Linguistically as well as psychologically, his complaint is bang on the money: the expression *faire tintin* means, as the dictionary of French slang points out, 'to be deprived of a satisfaction expected or due to one, to be frustrated in something'. *Tintin* is what happens to Sir Francis, and Tintin is the trauma of that event replaying for the Captain. Even his name contains a deadly repetition: Tin-tin – like the cars, the cows, the knights: *Tintin*, nothing, generalised collapse of all economies.

Tintin both offers and withholds. Long before Louis XIV and Sir Francis appear on the scene, he helps the Russian Kulaks stash away their wealth (tax-evade) *while* participating in the search for it. He is the master of the dummy-or double-chamber, of the double-dummy chamber. He uncovers (treasure) in order to hide (filiation), deciphers in order to help re-encrypt, marks in order to erase. He knows that the pearls that fall from Castafiore's necklace are fake ones, but hands them back to her, complicit. This perfect little exchange in *The Castafiore Emerald* serves as a miniature for the book's larger ones, and those beyond. His gesture on the cover – coy, knowing smile, raised eyebrows, finger pressed to lips – shows him for what he really is: a silencer, a guardian of the silence at the heart of all the noise. It also hints that, ultra-paradoxically, he is an *enabler* of all economies as well. Silencing, he allows the spectacle, the deal, the whole caboodle to continue by keeping its unspoken just that: unspoken.

Guardian of the silence at the heart of noise: as Barthes would put it, Tintin is the protector of the ultimate meaning held irretrievably in reserve; as Derrida would say, he is the avatar of the secret whose possibility guarantees the possibility of literature, the condition of this secret become visible. If, as sunflowers know, the secret of philosophy is literature, then what Hergé's whole *oeuvre*, in its silent medium, knows but will not allow to be pronounced, is that the secret of literature is Tintin.

6

A THING IN THE GRIP OF GRAVITY, OR, GLING, BLING, CLING

From *The Balloonatic*, Buster Keaton, 1923.

i

In the *Tintin* books, as we have seen, a process is being played out that is fundamental to the whole experience, the whole mode of literature. This process is dark, sometimes shocking, in many respects catastrophic, and perhaps even fatal. It is certainly sad. And yet it is played out to a large extent as comedy.

Hergé, like most people of his age and background, grew up in thrall to the films of Buster Keaton and Charlie Chaplin. His first ever comic strips, *Les Aventures de Totor, C.P. des hannetons*, which were published in the mid-twenties in *Le Boy-Scout Belge* and showed the exploits of a scout leader or *chef de patrouille* ('*C.P.*'), were framed by the announcement 'United Rovers presents a great comic film' and credited and 'copyrighted': 'Hergé Moving Pictures. Director: Hergé.' In these and then the *Tintin* strips themselves, Hergé, using a medium whose conventions were far from standardised, let cinema dictate the logic of his images' progression: the way the boxes follow one another in a line, like frames of film, each showing a still image of an instant coming after the one shown in the last box, thereby implying a continuum of movement through time. And cinema started with the gag: as Assouline points out, one of the first films ever made was the Lumière Brothers' 1896 *L'Arroseur Arrosé*, 'The Waterer Watered', whose title pretty much tells you what happens in it. It was silent, of course, but if it had had a dialogue this would probably have contained lines similar to those Haddock speaks as he tries to nail Abdullah with the hosepipe in *The Red Sea Sharks*.

The *Tintin* books are, of course, full of gags. They are also full of a more subtle kind of comedy that plays out in a social and psychological way, at the level of character and situation. But they are comic in a more philosophical sense too. For the great phenomenologist Henri Bergson, writing just as cinemas were springing up throughout Europe, the essence of comedy lies in the replacement of the natural by the mechanical. Life, he tells us in his 1911 work 'Laughter: An Essay on the Meaning of the Comic', is about uniqueness, singularity. When there is duplication, this rule is contravened, and comedy results. Bergson quotes his predecessor Pascal's dictum that 'Two faces that are alike, although neither of them excites laughter by itself, make us laugh when together, on account of their likeness.' For Bergson and Pascal, Thompson and Thomson are comic even before they mix their words up or bump into doors and lamp-posts. 'Analyse the impression you get from two faces that are too much alike,' writes Bergson, 'and you will find that you are thinking of two copies cast in the same mould, or two impressions of the same seal, or two reproductions of the same negative – in a word, of some manufacturing process or other. This deflection of life towards the mechanical is here the real cause of laughter.'

Here we are entering familiar territory: copies, seals, reproductions. It seems that the same thing that makes the *Tintin* books so anguished also makes them funny. For Bergson, it is not just reproduction that generates laughter: comedy occurs any time there is 'something mechanical encrusted on the living'. Mechanical stiffness of the body, rigidity overtaking the mobility of life, is funny: Haddock in his wheelchair in *The Castafiore Emerald*. A person being manipulated like an automaton by another person is funny: Tintin bending Haddock to his will by pulling out a bottle, getting him drunk and then suggesting that he is frightened of the yeti in order to pique him into resuming their search for Tchang in *Tintin in Tibet*, or simply pulling out a bottle in *The Red Sea Sharks* (whereupon we get a wonderful frame that quite literally shows us the cogs of Haddock's mind whirring). Any 'clockwork arrangement of human events' which 'conveys the impression of pure mechanism, of automatism, of movement without life' is funny: the rhythms of the house, its comings, going, bumpings, grindings, rings and chimes in *The Castafiore Emerald*.

Duplication, reproduction and automatism are funny, then. But what is funniest of all, claims Bergson, is repetition. Why? Again, because it is set against life itself, which is about uniqueness. The 'fundamental law of life' is 'the complete negation of repetition'. If I am watching someone talking and notice that 'a certain movement of head or arm, a movement always the same, seems to return at regular intervals, if I notice it and it succeeds in diverting my attention, if I wait for it to occur and it occurs when I expect it, then I involuntarily laugh'. Overall, the comic sensibility consists of 'looking at life as a repeating machine, with reversible and interchangeable parts', like a clock. Repetition, like duplication, is to do with the mechanical – but whereas duplication as a phenomenon applies to the realm of objects, repetition takes place in the field of time. Comedy, like film, unfolds through time, and turns time into a repeating mechanism. Abdullah understands comedy perfectly when, speaking like a film director, he tells Haddock: 'Again, Blistering Barnacle! Fall downstairs again!'

ii

Abdullah is onto something else here too, another aspect of the comic, perhaps the most simple one: the fall. According to Alan Dale, author of the 2000 study *Comedy is a Man in Trouble: Slapstick in American Movies*, the fall is pretty much *the* basic comic action. Baudelaire knew this already. In his 1855 essay 'The Essence of Laughter', which is full of examples of people slipping on ice and tripping on kerbstones, he writes that 'human laughter is intimately connected with the accident of an original fall, of a degradation both of the body and the mind'. Here, though, the fall has become more than simply a pratfall: it has theological overtones. A metaphysical dimension runs through Baudelaire's whole essay. He claims that laughter has a 'satanic' origin. God does not laugh; there is no laughter in Paradise. Our laughter, then, tells us that we are not in Paradise, that we are human. And this cuts both ways: on the one hand, it shows our 'infinite wretchedness by comparison with the absolute Being who exists as an idea in Man's mind', and on the other it shows our own 'infinite grandeur by comparison with the animals'. In this second respect, laughter is haughty, superior: 'I don't fall,' scoffs Baudelaire, 'I'm not the kind of fool who doesn't notice a break in the footpath, or a paving-stone blocking my way.' Within comedy this haughtiness is, of course, generally set up in order to be taken down again – set up, in other words, for a fall.

Captain Haddock not only falls at every opportunity, but he also keeps styling himself as someone who is above falling, thereby setting himself up even more to do just that. He warns Tintin and Nestor not to slip on the loose piece of marble on the staircase in *The Castafiore Emerald* and then slips on it himself. He lectures Nestor on the importance of being polite to ladies on the telephone and then loses his rag when one phones seconds later in *The Calculus Affair*. Time and again he turns his head to tell people to look where they are going and then crashes into whatever is in his path. Snowy does the same: 'Wake up, Tintin! Look where you're going!' he tuts at Tintin after the latter bumps into a lamp-post in *The Broken Ear* before, distracted by his tutting, he himself runs straight into a dustbin. Baudelaire might point out that Snowy is an animal – but he is one with very human qualities, especially in the early books, where he seems to hold functional two-way conversations with Tintin. If he seems slightly redundant in the later ones it is because he has been replaced by the

Captain, who not only takes over his characteristics (drunk-enness, clumsiness) but also has a propensity to lower himself to an animal level, arguing with parrots or llamas or the yeti who becomes his double.

The most emphatic instance of Haddock getting down with the animals is, of course, the scene in *The Seven Crystal Balls* in which he dons a pantomime cow's head and charges out onto the stage. This is (as they say of comedy) classic – in the classical sense: Haddock is playing Apuleius's Golden Ass or any number of half-man-half-animals from Ovid's *Metamorphoses* – or, fast-forwarding a few centuries, Shakespeare's Bottom, who in *A Midsummer Night's Dream* finds his head transformed into the head of an ass. 'Haddock, thou art translated!' But Haddock's continual falling, his numerous abasements, are also thoroughly Baudelairean, inasmuch as they testify to an infinite wretchedness. The Captain is, as he says of himself again and again, wretched: 'I'm a miserable wretch,' he sobs as Alan pours him a drink in *The Crab with the Golden Claws*; 'I'm a miserable wretch,' he splutters to Tintin hours later after burning their lifeboat's oars; 'I'm a miserable wretch,' he mumbles as he sobers up from his impromptu space-walk in *Explorers on the Moon*. That he is always falling, relapsing, messing up, is a sign of his awkward relationship not only with the material world but also with the divine one. More than once his gaffes interrupt reli-gious ceremonies: the Inca ritual, the Tibetan blessing. His clumsiness carries with it guilt: 'I'm sorry . . . I'm sorry!' 'I'm terribly sorry,' he says repeatedly to Tintin; to the Buddhist monks: 'Oh, sorry!'

As Hergé's collaborator (in all senses of the word) at *Le Soir* Paul de Man puts it in his 1969 essay 'The Rhetoric of Temporality', 'Baudelaire's falling man is a thing in the grip of gravity.' Tripping is not just about losing your equilibrium: it is also about existing in a universe which brings you down. Hergé understood this. The giant apples which tumble from the trees of his strange island in *The Shooting Star* are biblical and Newtonian at the same time. The moon books are full of gravity: the 'dreadful gravity' that makes the characters pass out on take-off and landing, the rocket's hatchways which Calculus, Haddock-like, keeps warning the others not to fall down before he falls down one himself – and, conversely, the sequences in which Haddock floats out of his boots and his whisky rolls into a ball and rises from the glass. If Hergé switches gravity off in these scenes, it is only in order to switch it on again and reassert it yet more forcefully: as the rocket's nuclear motor is restarted, Haddock crashes to the ground; his whisky splats across his face. Even Haddock's grandiose pontification at the book's end about man's proper place being here 'on dear old earth' is interrupted by a trip that pulls him flat onto it.

Dear old earth: for de Man, the fall within gravity is also a fall towards the grave. Gravity, like repetition, opens up the dimension of time, by testifying to 'the temporal reality of death'. This is what imposes itself on Hergé's characters in the asteroid sequence in *Explorers on the Moon*, in which the floating Haddock is sucked towards a giant rock against which, unless Calculus and Tintin can do something to counteract its gravity, he will eventually smash and be pulverised. The rock's name? Adonis. The sequence reads like a science-fiction rewrite of *Sarrasine* (or, indeed, *The Broken Ear*): Haddock, like the sculptor, is 'attracted by Adonis', 'pulled' into its 'dragging' orbit, and so is the rocket that is chasing after him, threatening the lives of all its crew, more and more with every passing minute. *Explorers on the Moon* is perhaps both the most wildly adventurous and the most contemplative of all the *Tintin* books. Taken allegorically, the Adonis episode seems to dramatise what is implicit elsewhere: that at the heart of all action lies the possibility of death, the same possibility that, for Balzac, lies beneath all attraction, like a force-field.

Thompson and Thomson are always falling: into the sea, off station platforms, even in the wards of hospitals. If it is not them falling then it is the ceiling that falls in on them: plaster, chandeliers. As Haddock tells them in the rocket, they are 'clowns' – classic ones of a type running back from Disney's Sorcerer's Apprentice to the servants Wagner in Marlowe's *Doctor Faustus* or Face in Ben Jonson's *The Alchemist*: half-witted juniors wandering around unsupervised in the master scientist's laboratory, misusing his equipment. In the final desert sequence of *Land of Black Gold* they find Müller's petrol-tampering pills lying around and eat them, making them burp and their hair grow uncontrollably. In *Destination Moon* they creep around the generating room, scaring themselves with the X-ray machine into believing that a malicious skeleton is loose in the Sprodj factory; finding another skeleton in the osteology department, they point their guns at it with trembling hands, arrest it, handcuff it and cart it away for questioning. Besides simply being farcical, the episode has other resonances: by choosing a skeleton as their quarry, it is almost as though Hergé were sending them off on a mission to arrest death itself. And this throws light, perhaps, on Thompson and Thomson's other frequent quarry, Tintin, who, despite his constant liaisons with death, despite being pronounced dead time and again and even repeatedly buried, never manages to stay dead. It may seem heroic that even when he is shot in the head, plunges into a waterfall, trips off a cliff or drops from a plane without a parachute he survives – but it could equally be seen as morbid.

Is the opposite of life artifice, death or un-death? At the beginning of *Sarrasine* an ancient la Zambinella, tottering around the de Lantys' party, is described in Bergsonian terms: as a 'fragile machine', an 'artificial creature' whose movements 'were accomplished only by means of some imperceptible artifice'. He is also, according to Barthes, beyond death. Why? Because he is beyond desire. 'The ultimate horror,' Barthes writes with a shudder, 'is not death but that the classification of death and life should be broken off.' Perhaps that is what undoes Thompson and Thomson every time, whether they are chasing the skeleton or Tintin: their failure to understand that death itself can never die.

iii

In tragedy, death confers meaning. The tragic hero rushes into death in order to make his or her life meaningful, to retroactively give it a significance of transcendental proportions. In comedy this option is removed. As Dale points out, Sylvester the Cat or Wile E. Coyote fall off cliffs and have bombs blow up in their face but never die. This is not to say that comedy produces no meaning. It does – but it is a different type of meaning, one that, paradoxically, is built on sadder, more long-suffering foundations.

Does this meaning have a name? Yes: irony. For Baudelaire, the one thing that distinguishes the artist and the philosopher from other humans is that they can laugh *at themselves*. They have the capacity to split themselves in two and be spectator of the fall as well as the one who falls. Baudelaire calls this *dédoublement*, 'doubling'. Bergson may see the duplication of other things or people as funny, but for Baudelaire comedy offers – only to a special few – *self*-duplication, *self*-multiplication. The problem is that, like the fetish, as soon as a person is duplicated or multiplied, they become fake – and then their artist's or philosopher's gift of self-awareness will only make them conscious of their own fakeness. And an awareness of one's own fakeness can have disastrous consequences. As de Man writes: 'The moment the innocence or authenticity of our sense of being in the world is put into question, a far from harmless process gets underway. It may start as a casual bit of play with a stray loose end of the fabric, but before long the entire texture of the self is unravelled and comes apart.'

The self-conscious laughter of the philosopher or artist, then, is the sound of their own disintegration – plus of their own recognition of their own disintegration. Yet another type of double-articulation lies at the heart of what de Man calls 'ironic language': this language, he says, splits the self into two selves, one of which is inauthentic and the other of which speaks of that inauthenticity. This does not, however, bring about a return to authenticity 'for', as he points out, 'to know inauthenticity is not the same as to be authentic'. This is the metaphysical condition of the man in the grip of irony: he may plead for salvation from it but he never gets it, and has to console himself with 'remembering' (or inventing) a pre-lapsarian era in which he was not fake. This, of course, opens up the field of time once more. 'Irony,' de Man declares with this fact in mind, 'divides the flow of temporal experience into a past that is pure mystification and a future that remains harassed forever by a relapse within the inauthentic. It can know inauthenticity but never overcome it. It can only restate and repeat it on an increasingly conscious level.'

Is this not the Captain's situation, his experience of time? He keeps finding himself trapped in inauthentic worlds. Amidst all the fake scenery backstage at the music hall in *The Seven Crystal Balls*, the door out to the 'real' world (via the 'bar', of course) turns out to be fake too, and slams him into a wall. His exit from the inauthentic world of the hotel room in *Tintin and the Picaros* is barred as well. There is something

Kafkaesque or Beckettian about his waiting day after day for the promised meeting with the general at which he will finally be able to 'explain' himself, to redeem himself back into clarity and truth. The meeting was never going to happen: the general was no more likely to show up than Godot. In this book's hotel room he is observed through two-way mirrors; in *The Calculus Affair* he contemplates himself in his own bathroom mirror. A small crack appears in the top corner, what de Man would call 'a stray loose end of the fabric'; then the whole mirror shatters and crashes to the floor; then the whole world of Marlinspike, a testament (if we know how to read it) to his fakeness, starts crumbling: GLING, BLING, CLING.

Captain Haddock, as we have seen in several contexts by now, is confronted time and again with his own inauthenticity. As the books progress the fact is stated more and more self-consciously. Haddock may never express it himself in so many words, but the situations in which he runs up against it face-to-face grow increasingly introspective: in *The Calculus Affair*, *The Castafiore Emerald* and *Tintin and the Picaros* the press come to report on it each time he is at home. Eventually it gets played out in the field of art, the most self-conscious of all environments. In *Tintin and Alph-Art* we see him staring awkwardly at the giant 'H' he has been lumped with ('H for Haddock, d'you get it?' he tells Tintin) – an artificial sign behind which lies a whole covert industry of fraudulence. Effectively, what he is looking at – or, rather, what *we*, through the double-language of irony Hergé has made his own, are looking at him looking at – is his condition.

Haddock's real name, we find out in *Tintin and the Picaros*, is Archibald. Adonis's is Irony. It is into irony's orbit that the Captain is dragged throughout Hergé's work, and with him is dragged the rest of the world of the *Tintin* books. He longs for redemption, but finds that every door that purports to offer him this merely leads – if it is a real door at all – into a wider world that is itself a testament to his inauthenticity. No space is outside irony for him, not even outer space. The sacred rituals that would redeem him from it are interrupted, often (irony of ironies) by his own efforts to participate in them. To turn water into wine would be a miracle. Death would be a release. Some peace and quiet to smoke his pipe in would be nice. Hergé sees to it that all these options will elude him.

For de Man, irony is a literary mode in which we see something fundamentally inherent to literature itself: its experience of time, of language and the world all revolving around the question of inauthenticity and various doomed attempts to overcome it. Other modes may be more bombastic, more intense, but irony seems to provide a channel that runs beneath all these, enabling them. In the music hall of *The Seven Crystal Balls*, several types of entertainment are put on display. Haddock has gone there, ostensibly, to see the most marvellous one. But he misses it and wanders around the wings where the scenery that goes to make up all the scenes is stored. That very scenery propels him into the main scene which, crashing in uninvited, he interrupts. Here, played out in the simplest form of comedy, slapstick, is the essence of Hergé's work in a single sequence. Taking place 'offstage' as far as the main 'scene' of literature is concerned, it, too, crashes in uninvited from the side, in all its silly clothes, embodying perfectly the ironic mode that forms literature's bass-note. If tragedy is literature's high Eucharist, its most sacred experience in which the self is transfigured and removed from time, then Hergé's work enacts the irony that transforms this ritual itself, leaving a taste that is neither water nor wine but, as Calculus (who with his alcohol aversion-inducing pills has made all Eucharists unconsumable) suspects in what turns out to be the complete *oeuvre*'s final line, mustard.

7

PIRATES!

'Détournements' of Tintin.

i

At the heart of Hergé's work, the backbone of the expanded story played out over twenty-four books and fifty years, lies a legacy: Sir Francis Haddock's legacy to his descendants. This legacy is interrupted, broken off, lost, refound, then lost and found again without ever being exhausted. Even when parchments have been overlaid and treasure unearthed, significant parts of it remain uncovered, as we have seen. The legacy brings with it a pattern of repetition: in the seventeenth century it is tied up in a story of bad, or partial, giving and non-recognition (by Louis to and of Sir Francis); in the twentieth, ditto (partial giving by Tintin to the Captain of a boat – one of three – and non-recognition by both men of the deeper situation in which they have involved themselves). In the seventeenth century the legacy picks up along its route a larger-than-life figure (the totemic statue of Sir Francis) whose voice booms throughout space and is even taken up by parrots, and yet whose ultimate message remains a silent one; in the twentieth century it picks up the formidable Bianca Castafiore, whom Hergé places right in front of the totem so that her voice can do the same. Legated in the seventeenth century, it divides into three parts which circulate through time and space until, eventually reunited in the twentieth, they repeat the act that brought the legacy about in the first place: the formation of an estate.

This is more than simply an extended plot device, of course. We have seen how it anchors deep concerns about ownership and possession that unfold on the mythic or symbolic scale via the theme of the stranger in the ancestral tomb and in a more modern or domestic way via that of the guest in the home. We have also seen how it is intimately tied in with Hergé's own family history. But the issue of ownership is also developed in another type of self-reflective way within the *Tintin* books, where Hergé uses it to play out anxieties surrounding creativity itself. In *The Calculus Affair* Professor Calculus's work is not only 'stolen' but also passed off as the work of Bordurian scientists. Even earlier, in *The Shooting Star*, the observatory's chief astronomer claims credit for the work of his long-suffering colleague-cum-assistant ('I, Decimus Phostle, have determined the moment at which the cataclysm will befall us! Tomorrow I shall be famous!' he cries after the subordinate hands him his calculations and informs him that the meteor collision 'will take place at 0812 hours and 30 seconds precisely'). In that book, the question of rightful ownership becomes less clear-cut when a fragment of the meteor shears off and lands in the ocean: like genius itself, it has come from elsewhere and, once it has emerged, is up for grabs. It must be claimed through a back-and-forth tussle: Aurora versus Peary, Europe versus (South) America.

Throughout the *Tintin* books, each project has a counter-project. The Sprodj rocket-base must grapple with the agents of 'some unknown Power' which wants to bring the rocket back to a base in its country, hoard the research Calculus and the others have carried out and claim for itself the glory of having put a mission on the moon. Tintin's quest for the fetish is mirrored step by step by that of Ramón and Alonso who, no fools, make the same deductions as him at roughly the same time. The m'Hatouvou tribe vie with the Babaoro'm, the Rumbabas with the Arumbayas, Alcazar with Tapioca, *Paris-Flash* with *Tempo di Roma*. The need to possess – or, perhaps more accurately, not to be dispossessed – is often so strong that each side would rather see the contested object destroyed than have it fall into their rival's hands: Calculus blows up his own rocket and Sir Francis his own boat. This second contested object will lie dormant for centuries before coming up for grabs and starting the tussle all over again. The latter-day tussle is, of course, resolved in favour of Haddock and his entourage, who consolidates his ancestral estate in winning it. Look how resolutely he defaces the poster announcing Marlinspike's availability: 'This home is *NOT* for sale.' He even, like Hergé copyrighting his cartoons, signs it triumphantly with his own proper name: 'Signed: Haddock.'

Does Haddock win his inheritance back because he has a proper moral right to it, whereas the Bird Brothers and the other potential buyers do not? Because Haddock is the rightful descendant of Sir Francis? What about his other descendants? He had three sons: there must be heaps of

Haddocks running about by now. No, the reason Haddock wins 'his' home 'back' is that Calculus invents a shark-sub-marine and sells it to the government – that is, to the military (despite his protestations to the contrary, he has no qualms about developing weapons so long as he is credited and paid for it). As soon as we examine them more closely, the contingency of 'natural' processes of inheritance emerges. Look at the way Tintin acquires eventual possession of all three parchments in *The Secret of the Unicorn*: by taking Max Bird's wallet, which contains two of them, from the pickpocket who stole it and then getting Thompson and Thomson to bring him the third, again from Bird, when they arrest the antiques dealer. This is extremely dubious practice, to say the least. The 'correct' procedure would be to return the two wallets to Bird, criminal or not, enter a claim for them and let justice run its course. But Tintin takes it and gets away with taking it, because Thompson and Thomson not only fail to intervene and stop him but also actively help him in his plundering. Justice is on his side; it works for him.

ii

Concerns over the issue of ownership play themselves out *in* the *Tintin* books, and they also play themselves out *around* the *Tintin* books. As his work grew more and more successful,

Hergé came to acquire a large staff of assistants. They would certainly have seen a nod in their direction when Calculus shows Haddock the rows of people working at their drawing boards in *Destination Moon*. Hergé's assistants became so good at drawing his characters that the difference between his own rendition and theirs grew indiscernible. Even before this era, for *The Seven Crystal Balls* and *Prisoners of the Sun* he relied so much on the collaboration of fellow cartoonist Edgar Jacobs that when the time came for publication Jacobs requested to co-sign. Hergé refused and the two men fell out. Right to the end he signed the books 'Hergé' rather than 'Studios Hergé' – and let it be widely understood that, whereas 'Disney' denoted a huge corporate operation, 'Hergé' meant him and only him. During the final year or so of his life, muted discussions took place about whether or not the books would continue when he was no longer around to author them. One of his most senior assistants, Bob de Moor, was keen to take on the mantle and produce more adventures, and was bitterly disappointed to discover that he would not be permitted to do this. When several people proposed to his widow after his death that *Tintin and Alph-Art* be either completed or at least fully rendered according to Hergé's sketches, she considered this but, following his express wishes, refused to grant permission.

Illegitimate versions of both this adventure and other, apocryphal ones flourished, though. Some of these purported to be bona fide *Tintin* books; others engaged in a practice known as *détournement*. Popularised by the Situationist leader Guy Debord (the theorist of the 'Society of the Spectacle' whom we met earlier), *détournement* involves the taking over of a sign, image, text or body of work and the redirecting of it to one's own ends. Indeed, Debord's own vehicle, the magazine *Situationist International,* featured in 1973 a 'détourned' version of *The Crab with the Golden Claws*'s cover, replacing the word 'Crab' with 'Capital'. Hergé's work has been 'détourned' so many times that a thorough survey of this would take up a whole book itself. Generally speaking, though, *détournements* of Tintin break down into three categories: pornographic ones, in which the characters go around getting laid and screwing one another (as in Jan Bucquoy's 1992 *La Vie Sexuelle de Tintin,* an image from which can be seen on page 180); political ones, in which Tintin lends his talents to some cause or other, such as Irish Republicanism, Central American Communism or London Anarchism (as in J. Daniels's 1989 *Breaking Free,* an excerpt from which can also be seen on page 180); and 'art' ones. Among the more interesting recent offerings from this third camp are Australian artist Alex Hamilton's 2000 *Flame Book,* in which the box-frame sequence from *The Calculus Affair* is reproduced exactly, all sixty-two pages of it, with the boxes emptied of their original text and drawings and filled instead with a single, repeating image of flames; and the French artist Jochen Gerner's 2002 *TNT en Amérique* (a page of which is reproduced on page 2), in which, nodding in the direction of Bataille's concept of 'deformation', the artist eclipses almost all of *Tintin in America* with black ink, leaving only a few symbols (mainly of violence, commerce or divinity) and words to serve as memorials to what has been buried.

Détournements of *Tintin* predate even Debord. After the liberation in September 1944, the Belgian newspaper *La Patrie* published the crudely drawn strip *Tintin au Pays des Nazis* or 'Tintin in the Land of the Nazis' as a way of ostracising Hergé. What is most interesting about the couple of short episodes this ran to (one of which is shown on page 180) is that Tintin and Haddock themselves remain goodies in them, denouncing their creator before setting off to look for German V2s. Another interesting episode to occur during Hergé's lifetime was the publication, in the late fifties and early sixties, of pirate versions of *Tintin in the Land of the Soviets*. The memory of this adventure, which had never appeared in colour or even been reprinted since before the war, continued to make him a hate-figure among certain sectors of the left for long after its publication, and after the war he had wanted it to simply sink from view – effectively, to 'unclaim' it as his work. But when the pirate versions came out they were of such bad graphic quality that he decided he should save his reputation as a draftsman, if not his new-found one as a leftist, and let Casterman publish the album properly.

Nor are the practices of piracy and *détournement* limited to ones that steal or bend Hergé's work to produce new work elsewhere. They are already going on *within* the work. From *The Blue Lotus* onwards Hergé was so devoted to the task of getting detail right that he would lift backgrounds and scenes from books and magazines. But his lifting began even earlier than this. The hero of Benjamin Rabier's turn-of-the-century illustrated poems *Tintin-Lutin*, a young boy with a tuft and a dog, is so close in both name and appearance to Tintin that Hergé's work could justifiably be described as a *détournement* of Rabier's from its very outset. The same claim could be made about the relation between *Tintin* and Hector Malot's late nineteenth-century adventure *Sans Famille*, 'Without Family', whose hero, 'Remi' (no less), is born of aristocrats but raised by peasants. He, too, has a dog, named 'Capi' (short for *Capitaine*), and an enemy named Allen. And to top it all, the ancestral home to which he eventually returns is called 'Milligan' – 'mill' like the French *moulin*, the main stem of *Moulinsart* or Marlinspike. If you cannot find these books, go and read Jules Verne's 1868 adventure *Children of Captain Grant* and his 1870 one *Around the Moon*: suffice to say that you will do a double-take when you come to the condor hang-gliding and floating whisky scenes.

As T. S. Eliot said: 'Bad writers imitate; good writers steal.' The American novelist William Burroughs published in 1985 a whole manifesto based on this belief, urging artists of all types to abandon what he called 'the fetish of originality': 'Bosch, Michelangelo, Renoir, Monet, Picasso – steal anything in sight. You want a certain light on your scene? Lift it from Monet. You want a 1930s backdrop? Use Hopper.' Pointing out that Joseph Conrad wrote some superb descriptive passages on jungles, water and weather, Burroughs suggests: 'why not use them verbatim in a novel set in the tropics? Continuity by so-and-so, description and background footage from Conrad.' Shakespeare's *Romeo and Juliet* has been served up so many times, he reasons, why not just be honest and keep their names? Shakespeare would have chuckled reading this as, being way ahead of the game here as in most other areas, he was doing this from the word go. Earlier versions of *Macbeth* and *King Lear* already existed when he wrote the plays: he took the titles, characters and plot lines from these. For *Julius*

Caesar he lifted whole speeches from the Roman equivalent of *Hansard*, leaving parts of them untouched and modifying others as he saw fit. In short, he 'détourned'.

All literature is pirated. Good literature is constantly expropriated, reappropriated and remade – both by other writers *and* by readers. Every act of reading is its own kind of remaking of a work: everyone will have their own experience of a book, and no two of these experiences will ever be the same. Perhaps a portion of the anxiety exuded by the trial-rocket sequence in *Destination Moon,* in which Calculus cries and tears his hair out as the rocket slips from his remote-control grasp into that of the other camp, can be ascribed to the writer–reader relationship: Calculus, like Hergé or any other author, has launched his work into the world at large which, after the close proximity in which he has held it for so long, must seem as large as outer space, sent it beyond the bounds of his control. Sir Francis's parchments are like the rocket in that respect: missiles or missives sent through time rather than space, texts which will be read by generations who were not even conceived when they were written. Sir Francis's sons were such bad readers that they did not even manage to follow the instructions in their father's will which would have led them to the parchments. Tintin and Haddock are better readers, but they still miss what is occluded in the parchments' text, written between its lines. Ultimately, though, this does not matter: what is important for the adventure's continuation is not that they get it 'right' but rather that it opens up a space for readings to take place in – and to be contested, grabbed and counter-grabbed. All grabbers on the high seas of literature are pirates: some, like Sir Francis – or Tintin – have, through one means or another, acquired the seal of 'legitimacy'.

iii

Which brings us to the question of Hergé's estate – 'estate' in its strict legal sense of legacy, of rights of 'ownership' legated after death. Hergé was infertile, as we have already seen, and left no heir. After he died, his second wife Fanny married a much younger English man named Nick Rodwell, where-upon the sequence in *Tintin in America* in which Tintin is engulfed by marketing men eager to exploit his image ('Ten thousand dollars for Snowy's picture in our Doggie Dinner: "I win the tricks with Bonzo Bix, says Super-Sleuth Snowy!"') sprang off the page and into life. Under Rodwell's guidance, the 'Fondation Hergé' consolidated the rights to virtually all images of Tintin, while its sister company Moulinsart exploited these commercially through T-shirts, duvet covers, coffee cups and who knows what else (if they were really on the ball they might actually license a dog food brand called Bonzo Bix and adorn it with Snowy's image). Fiercely pro-tective of their assets, the Fondation and Moulinsart have been known to set their lawyers onto independent web sites devoted to Tintin and to suppress free and open discussion of, for example, Hergé's wartime activities by withholding image rights from critics and biographers who err into this subject's minefield. As Georges Remi Jr, Hergé's nephew who inherited his name but nothing else, writes, 'The boat has been taken over and the red flag raised . . . Oh my poor uncle, "they" have really done you over!'

The occasional 'legitimate' adaptation of *Tintin* is allowed: a product-placement-friendly theatre-play for children here, an animated cartoon set for TV there. As this book goes to press, a major project is being planned, a film by Steven Spielberg. Hergé met Spielberg shortly before his death and the two men discussed doing this, but Spielberg's copyright demands were so excessive that the deal fell through, and Spielberg went off and made *Raiders of the Lost Ark*, with all its scenes of penetrated tombs and cursed, death-giving fetishes. After several posthumous rounds of negotiation, though, it seems the project is back on the rails. It will be interesting to see what love interest Spielberg gives his Tintin.

Exercising iron control over an estate and milking it for all it is worth are not limited to the Fondation Hergé-Moulinsart. The work of many of the twentieth century's major artists and writers now finds itself wrapped up in legal barbed wire. The estate of James Joyce, who saw 'litterature' itself as rich trash to be recycled and adapted and who spent months on end reading the notes and correspondence of previous great writers in public libraries, is positively draconian when it comes to authorising adaptations or allowing access to material. That of T. S. Eliot, who made a career out of reusing other people's lines, stamps down on any citation of his work that exceeds the amount the letter of the law allows. Academics fulminate at this and cry for changes in the copyright laws (which currently protect work for seventy years after its author's death). Artists, meanwhile, do what artists always did: steal. Perhaps when the end of *Tintin*'s protection era comes the period will be viewed nostalgically by creative people who want to base their work on Hergé's as a golden age, a time when it still had the *frisson* of illegality. The really savvy ones are not bothering themselves about that now, though: if they have any sense they are involving themselves in the planning of an opera set to open on 3 March 2053. Its title? *The Castafiore Emerald*.

Why an opera? Hergé disliked the medium. He tells Sadoul: 'I see the fat lady behind the singer, even if she has an admirable voice, the buck behind the tenor, the papier-mâché of the décors, the tin of the swords, the cotton-wool beards of the chorus who shout "Let us go, let us go, let us go . . ." without moving an inch.' In other words, he finds that its fake nature breaks through its studied surface – which makes it a perfect medium through which to play out the themes and anxieties active in the *Tintin* books. It is a garish, unrealistic, 'silly' medium – all the better.

As an opera, *The Castafiore Emerald* follows the plot of the book pretty faithfully. In its first scene, Haddock and Tintin wander through woods whose magpies and squirrels chirp and chatter melodically while the Captain sings in a deep voice about the joys of spring – until a sour, discordant note is struck as both he and Tintin smell a rubbish dump on which gypsies have pitched their camp. Shrill piccolos announce the presence of Miarka in the woods; clashing cymbals and bellowing trombones accompany her biting of Haddock. When she is reunited with the gypsy troupe, the opera's first major aria is sung: 'You must be careful (I see a carriage)', in which a fortune-teller warns the Captain of events lurking in his near future. The Captain responds with his own aria, 'Mumbo-jumbo (Let go of my hand)', snatches his hand away from her and leaves – but not before, singing of the benefits of hospitality, he invites the gypsies to move onto the meadow on his estate.

The second scene moves at a quicker pace. We have thuds, ringing phones, arriving telegrams, and even a foretaste of the opera's main aria 'Ah, je ris!' (plagiarised straight from Gounod) when the Captain, imitating the famous diva Bianca Castafiore who has made the song her own, sings a strain of it while mixing himself a whisky. Discovering from one of the telegrams that the very same Castafiore is descending on him uninvited, Haddock orders Nestor to pack his bags, singing 'Let us go, let us go, let us go . . .' while moving in a panicked and yet painfully slow loop towards the door and back to the centre of the stage each time Tintin reads him an update of Castafiore's arrival time. When he finally does manage to leave the stage, a loud bass-drum roll with a few tings on a triangle thrown in for good measure signals that he has slipped on the same staircase he has just admonished Nestor against slipping on. A doctor informs him he has twisted his ankle; Castafiore arrives and Act One draws to a close.

The first scene of Act Two is given over to Haddock's Parrot Dream, in which row upon row of tuxedoed parrots stare in disapproval at his nakedness while a Castafiore-parrot sings snatches of the very Gounod aria he was mimicking – snatches that, forming part of a dream, distort, play themselves backwards and mutate into accounts of pirates, kings and covenants, all of which objects and personae obligingly appear and float above his bed (it is in this scene that we first see the carved idol of the ancestor, with his large open mouth). Act Two's second scene consists of a complex sound-collage formed by first alternating and then overlaying scales played on a piano winched down onto the stage during the scene itself with more ringing phones offset by the voice of a real parrot imitating them, these two and a half sources themselves being perfectly counter-balanced and yet teetering on the edge of cacophony when set against the scene's other musical sources: doorbells, shrill, modulating laughter, cries of 'I can hear you!', scales, more phones, more scales.

Act Two, scene three, the soon-to-be famous 'Garden Scene', consists of a long duet whose protagonists drop out, are replaced, then reappear like members of a tag-wrestling team as it progresses. Its first phase is sung by Calculus and a jour-nalist, each speaking at cross-purposes; its second by Calculus and la Castafiore; its third by Haddock and la Castafiore; its fourth by Tintin and the diva; and its fifth, angry one by Calculus and the now red-nosed Haddock. After a light inter-lude provided by the Marlinspike Prize Band in Act Two, scene four, the opera's most ambitious act gets under way.

Act Three is given over in its entirety to the filming – or attempted filming – of la Castafiore by a television crew. The technical requirements for its *mise-en-scène* are huge: fully operational cameras to relay a closed-circuit image to a set of television monitors also mounted on stage; a sound technician whose recorded fragments of sung dialogue are played back in *contrapunto* to the live libretto itself; electrical cables which, carrying real current, have to first function and then cut out at the correct moment to provide a blackout. In fact, the whole production's technical requirements are prodigious. Its composer has specified that a real parrot must be used but that its lines must be 'ventriloquised' for it from an offstage speaker. What the composer did not anticipate was that as the rehearsals progressed the parrot would start repeating both its and the humans' lines at all the wrong moments, wreaking havoc with the cueing system. Rumour among the opera world has it that the difficulties encountered with the parrot during rehearsals have been as nothing compared to those posed by the capriciousness of the real diva playing la Castafiore, who has demanded to be provided with genuine jewels as props, claiming not to be able to muster the passion to sing Gounod's 'Ah, je ris!' unless she has at least one actual emerald in front of her – this despite reports in the Italian press (which she has consequently banned from access to the opera house in which the production is being staged, although security, it must be said, is pretty lax) that the pearls which adorn her own neck are false.

The production has been so beset with trouble that the *figurants* or professional 'extras', generally suspicious types, have begun to murmur among themselves that it is cursed. Only three days before the opening night the director twisted his ankle while demonstrating to the baritone playing Captain

Haddock how to demonstrate to the tenor playing Nestor and the counter-tenor playing Tintin how not to trip on the newly laid stair while greeting Bolt the builder when the set designer who had just laid the stair appeared at the door in Bolt's place to warn the director to warn the cast not to step on it. A warning might have been redundant anyhow, as the cast do not seem to take on board anything the director tells them – not least the Prize Band musicians, whom he suspects have been using their stage-drunkenness as a cover under which to remain genuinely drunk throughout rehearsals. Meanwhile, the diva playing Castafiore has kept losing the emerald she has obligingly been provided with and then, after rehearsals have been halted and the police summoned, finding it again, only to mislay it the next day. The props manager is not that worried: he knows it is fake.

And so on. All of which have gone to make *The Castafiore Emerald* the most widely talked-about and eagerly anticipated production to hit the stage in a long time. The opera house is jam-packed for the opening night: tickets long ago sold out. The orchestra has finished tuning. The lead violinist has taken his seat and the conductor his bow. As he turns to his players the fire curtain draws back to reveal another, thin curtain behind it – one on which is printed a huge pair of effeminate lips and, held to them, a single finger. It seems that these lips themselves are speaking, or being spoken for, when the audience's murmur gives over to a set of whispers that, rising from several places in the stalls, blur into one as they float upwards, past the boxes: 'Shhh!'

SUGGESTIONS FOR FURTHER READING

Abraham, Nicolas and Torok, Maria, *The Wolf Man's Magic Word: A Cryptonymy*, trans. Nicholas Rand (University of Minnesota Press, 1986).

Anonymous, *The Thousand and One Nights*, trans. N. J. Dawood (Penguin Classics, 1973).

Aristotle, *Poetics*, trans. Malcolm Heath (Penguin Books, 1997).

Bachelard, Gaston, *The Poetics of Space*, trans. Maria Jolas (Beacon Press, 1994).

Balzac, Honoré de, *Sarrasine* in Roland Barthes's *S/Z (An Essay)*, trans. Richard Miller (Hill and Wang, 1975).

Barthes, Roland, *S/Z (An Essay)*, trans. Richard Miller (Hill and Wang, 1975).

Bataille, Georges, *Literature and Evil*, trans. Alastair Hamilton (Marion Boyars, 2001).

——, *Visions of Excess: Selected Writings 1927–1939*, trans. Allan Stoekl (University of Minnesota Press, 1985).

Baudelaire, Charles, *The Essence of Laughter*, trans. Gerard Hopkins (Meridian Books, 1956).

Bergson, Henri, *Laughter. An Essay on the Meaning of the Comic*, trans. Cloudesley Brereton (Dover Editions, 2005).

Blanchot, Maurice, *The Gaze of Orpheus and Other Literary Essays*, trans. Lydia Davis (Station Hill Press, 1981).

Burroughs, William, *Les Voleurs* in *The Adding Machine* (John Calder, 1985).

Conrad, Joseph, *Heart of Darkness* (Penguin Books, 2000).

de Man, Paul, *The Rhetoric of Temporality* in *Blindness and Insight* (University of Minnesota Press, 1983).

Derrida, Jacques, *Given Time: 1. Counterfeit Money*, trans. Peggy Kamuf (University of Chicago Press, 1994).

——, *White Mythology: Metaphor in the Text of Philosophy* in *Margins of Philosophy*, trans. Alan Bass (University of Chicago Press, 1984).

Duhamel, Georges, *America the Menace: Scenes from the Life of the Future*, trans. Charles Miner Thompson (George Allen and Unwin, 1930).

Freud, Sigmund, *Notes on a Case of Obsessional Neurosis (The Wolf Man)* in *Case Histories II*, trans. James Strachey (Penguin Books, 1991).

Home, Stewart (ed.), *What is Situationism? A Reader* (AK Press, 1996).

Mauss, Marcel, *The Gift: The Form and Reason for Exchange in Archaic Societies*, trans. W. D. Halls (W. W. Norton and Company, 2000).

McKeon, Michael, *The Origins of the English Novel 1600–1740* (Johns Hopkins University Press, 2002).

Plato, *The Sophist*, trans. Seth Bernadette (University of Chicago Press, 1986).

Pynchon, Thomas, *Gravity's Rainbow* (Penguin Classics, 1995).

Shakespeare, William, *The Sonnets* (Cambridge University Press, 2006).

——, *Macbeth* (Arden, 1997).

——, *The Tempest* (Arden, 1999).

——, *King Lear* (Arden, 1997).

In French only

Apostolidès, Jean-Marie, *Les Métamorphoses de Tintin* (Seghers, 1984).

Assouline, Pierre, *Hergé* (Gallimard, 1998).

Douillet, Joseph, *Moscou sans Voiles: Neuf ans de travail au pays des Soviets* (Paris, 1928).

Gerner, Jochen, *TNT en Amerique* (L'Ampoule, 2002).

Peyrefitte, Roger, *Tableaux de Chasse, ou, La vie extraordinaire de Fernand Legros* (Albin Michel, 2006).

Sadoul, Numa, *Entretiens avec Hergé: Tintin et moi* (Casterman, 1983).

Serres, Michel, *Hermès 2: L'interférence* (Editions de Minuit, 1980).

Tisseron, Serge, *Tintin et les Secrets de Famille* (Séguier, 1990); *Tintin et le Secret d'Hergé* (Presses de la Cité, 1993).

INDEX